A New Alliance:
Continuous Quality and Classroom Effectiveness

by Mimi Wolverton

ASHE-ERIC Higher Education Report No. 6, 1994

D1198764

Prepared by

Clearinghouse on Higher Education
The George Washington University

In cooperation with

Association for the Study
of Higher Education

Published by

Graduate School of Education and Human Development
The George Washington University

Jonathan D. Fife, Series Editor

Cite as

Wolverton, Mimi. 1994. *A New Alliance: Continuous Quality and Classroom Effectiveness.* ASHE-ERIC Higher Education Report No. 6. Washington, D.C.: The George Washington University, School of Education and Human Development.

Library of Congress Catalog Card Number 96-075835
ISSN 0884-0040
ISBN 1-878380-62-1

Managing Editor: Bryan Hollister
Manuscript Editor: Alexandra Rockey
Cover design by Michael David Brown, Rockville, Maryland

The ERIC Clearinghouse on Higher Education invites individuals to submit proposals for writing monographs for the *ASHE-ERIC Higher Education Report* series. Proposals must include:
1. A detailed manuscript proposal of not more than five pages.
2. A chapter-by-chapter outline.
3. A 75-word summary to be used by several review committees for the initial screening and rating of each proposal.
4. A vita and a writing sample.

ERIC Clearinghouse on Higher Education
School of Education and Human Development
The George Washington University
One Dupont Circle, Suite 630
Washington, DC 20036-1183

This publication was prepared partially with funding from the Office of Educational Research and Improvement, U.S. Department of Education, under contract no. ED RR-93-0200. The opinions expressed in this report do not necessarily reflect the positions or policies of OERI or the Department.

EXECUTIVE SUMMARY

Continuous quality improvement (CQI) first moved onto
the education scene slightly more than ten years ago. Some
institutions of higher learning—community colleges in particular—eagerly embraced its general precepts. Most tried
to ignore CQI and it greatest advocate, the American business
community. At best, a handful of stalwart organizations reluc-
tantly tested CQI's applicability in administrative areas and
student support services. Few colleges or universities ventured
onto the academic turf of faculty and into their classrooms.
Convinced that continuous quality was one more passing
fancy, many faculty seemed content to wait it out. Now, ten
years later, CQI is still with us, and while skepticism remains
high, examples do exist of sustained CQI endeavors in higher
education in which considerable inroads have been made
into the classroom.

What Is Continuous Quality Improvement?

The principles of CQI rest on an underlying philosophy of
quality, which leads an organization to regularly review how
it operates in order to find areas that need to be upgraded
or changed. Organizational members make decisions based
on more than supposition, consciously determine who holds
a vested interest in what the organization does (in and outside
the organization), and actively seek input from the various
groups of stakeholders. The organization establishes policies,
which encourage innovation and risk taking. It removes organizational barriers by establishing clear and open lines of
communication. It views learning as a continual process and
provides its members with ongoing professional development
opportunities, and it fosters a collegial working environment.
In other words, CQI provides a structure amenable to sustained and orderly change that is designed to improve the
organization through collaborative efforts (Coate 1990;
Cornesky et al. 1990, 1991; Gitlow and Gitlow 1987;
Seymour 1992).

In education, students became the focus, classroom effectiveness the concern, and assessment the means by which
educators gain feedback about what works and what needs
to be improved. Under continuous quality, a college or university seeks to increase the quality of all phases of the educational experience that it offers. The ultimate goal is to
enhance classroom effectiveness to improve student learning

(Carlson and Awkerman 1991; Chaffee and Sherr 1992; Deming 1982; Seymour 1992).

What Are the Examples?

This report looks at classroom-related CQI efforts at six institutions. Two organizations hold research one status, two are comprehensive universities, and two are community colleges.

The quality initiative in the Graduate School of Business at the University of Chicago is faculty driven. It concentrates heavily on classroom assessment and personal improvement through the use of quality principles. Although the school's quality effort began in the late 1980s, it remains unintegrated across the school.

At the College of Business at Arizona State University, CQI has been introduced collegewide by the dean. It combines active learning and some teaming within the frame that the quality principles provide and involves both curricular and pedagogical revisions.

A small group of faculty introduced CQI to the College of Engineering at Arizona State University. Their approach includes a required freshman course on active learning, assessment, team training, and total quality management, or TQM. Competency-based grading, which centers on cognitive and affective levels of learning, remains a highly contested element among large numbers of the faculty.

The Culture of Quality at Northwest Missouri State University began to take shape in 1984. Under the direction of Northwest's president, faculty concentrate on the processes of developing curriculum and assessing teaching and learning experiences using quality principles.

Both the president and the provost at Samford University saw merit in the university's embarking on its Student-First Quality Quest. This program cuts across the entire university. Faculty regularly use CQI tools like cause-and-effect diagrams and Pareto and flowcharts to diagnose curricular needs. Trained student teams conduct term evaluations of some courses.

In 1992 after a one-year pilot program at Rio Salado Community College (a Maricopa College), the chancellor of the district moved Maricopa into Quantum Quality. Implementation has been most successful at Rio Salado, where there is a heavy emphasis on TQM training for faculty and staff. Other campuses are experiencing mixed levels of involvement.

Miami-Dade Community College is a non-CQI institution, which some refer to as an exemplar of TQM. Its president-intitated, faculty-directed Teaching/Learning Project includes a reward system that uses teaching portfolios and a professional development program structured around advancement criteria that relate to classroom effectiveness. Classroom assessment plays a major role in Miami-Dade's efforts to improve student learning.

What Are the Common Threads?
Each institution views its students as the primary stakeholder group being served, and there is a heightened awareness of their needs. Initiatives with the greatest faculty involvement are those in which top administrators actively participate in the reform. Each college or university customized its faculty development offerings to meet its own specific requirements. Most combined active learning, CQI (under one name or another), and teaming. All included classroom assessment as a key element. Each institution either realigned current fiscal resources or found new sources of funding to accommodate the considerable financial expenditure that accompanied their moves into CQI. People at all the colleges and universities seem to understand that change takes time.

What Are Some of the Lingering Misgivings about CQI?
Standardization. Professional schools, such as business and engineering, seem to have success at setting standards. This may be the case because the competencies that their students must learn more readily lend themselves to measurement than do those needed by students of subjects like creative writing and anthropology. In areas like these, who defines quality and who sets standards that are measurable?

Benchmarking and customer focus. Benchmarking and meeting customer needs are both cornerstones of CQI. But does setting our sights on goals, based on even the most current information, give us enough freedom and flexibility to see the future? Will colleges and universities ensconced on the register of CQI organizations relegate themselves to the perpetual role of the want-to-be follower? If an organization decides to be an exemplar for others, can it lead yet continually gauge its progress by where it sits in relationship to its peers?

Teams. Teams take time, training, and energy; they do not just happen. Grouping people and assuming that they will work together productively often scuttles the best of intentions. We forget to ask the obvious: Do faculty and students know how to work in teams? And if the answer is no, do we have the impetus to teach them?

Quality. CQI organizations continually improve the quality of the processes in which they engage on a daily basis. In effect, the challenge becomes doing what we already do— only better. Rarely do we question what we do. In a future filled with financial uncertainty, greater public scrutiny and more calls for accountability, exponentially exploding knowledge bases, and increasingly diverse constituencies, we must ask: Is CQI enough?

CONTENTS

FOREWORD

During the middle of a semester, have you ever begun to question what was going on in the classroom? Have you ever rasied such questions as:

- Why do I teach my class the way I do?
- What results do I really want to achieve with my teaching?
- How do I know I am getting these results in both the short and long terms?
- Do I always have to guess at how well my students are learning until I give them the final exam?

If you have, the journey has begun for introducing quality into the classroom. Many faculty think that since quality principles (also known as total quality management, or TQM, continuous quality improvement, or CQI, total quality leadership, or TQL, or, as Pat Cross describes it, something like it, or SLI) originated within business, they have no place within education. However, these principles are not merely business techniques but rather fundamental ways to solve problems and ensure effectiveness in all facets of personal and professional life. The chairman of Toyota describes the quality process as "thinking why something is done and why it is done that way, then thinking differently to improve it."

Whether it is called a state of quality, or excellence, or just a "darn good" professional performance, three basic conditions or considerations must be present for long-term, effective results to occur. First is the belief that for any activity, especially those related to an occupation considered a "profession," there must be standards. These standards or outcomes cannot occur accidentally but should be thoughtfully defined and purposefully achieved. To do so requires a clear idea about these standards and how to recognize when these standards are being or have been achieved.

After accepting the principle of professional standards, the second consideration is a willingness to be held accountable by establishing ways to know, within a certain range of tolerance, if the standards are being achieved. While a degree of "professional judgment" will always play a part in this assessment, there is the need to establish direct and measurable links between the desired outcomes and the achievements.

The third and more subtle consideration is the recognition that every action has an effect on something else. In fact, if a professional outcome such as learning is to occur, it is expected that the action of the teacher will have an impact on the student, who in turn will respond in such a way as to influence the actions of the teacher. When teaching and learning are understood as an interactive, interrelated, and interdependent continuous process, then the need to monitor the process becomes as important as assessing the accomplishment of the student at the end of the process.

Thus, the three principles of quality—recognizing the need for teaching standards, being willing to be held accountable to these standards through measurable outcomes, and understanding that equal attention must be placed on the teaching/learning process and the outcomes—are not new or contrary to academic professional values. Indeed, they provide a new way to become more effective as a faculty member.

When the interrelated and interdependent nature of the classroom is understood, it is easy to recognize that the teaching/learning process is always changing. Factors such as the training and teaching skill of the professor, the prior academic preparation of the student, the adequacy of the teaching materials, and the various learning styles of the students all influence the success of the classroom. Factors such as these are changing constantly from class to class and semester to semester. Therefore, faculty must continuously monitor the process and make timely adjustments. This awareness of the need for continuous improvement and the provision of tools and techniques to accomplish a greater level of professional effectiveness that is afforded by the quality principles have helped to create a new alliance between the classroom and the techniques of continuous quality.

In this report by Mimi Wolverton, an assistant professor in the Department of Educational Leadership and Counseling Psychology at Washington State University, the concept of TQM and the implications of the Malcolm Baldrige National Quality Award education pilot criteria are briefly reviewed. This overview is followed by an examination of the experiences of seven organizations as they worked to improve the effectiveness of the classroom through the integration of the quality principles with the teaching and learning process. Dr. Wolverton concludes by relating the experiences of these institutions to seven basic questions concerning the use of the quality principles.

During the last decade, academic and political leaders have been calling for evidence that higher education is effectively meeting not only the expectations of society but also the claims asserted by the faculty. Increasingly, faculty are accepting responsibility for more accountability for their professional performance. This report is part of the evidence that the principle of quality will greatly aid faculty to demonstrate to others that they are effectively achieving high teaching standards while maintaining professional control and integrity within their classrooms.

Jonathan D. Fife
Series Editor, Professor of Higher Education, and
Director, ERIC Clearinghouse on Higher Education

ACKNOWLEDGMENTS

I wish to express my thanks to Dick Richardson, who had faith in my ability and suggested that I undertake such a project; to Jonathan Fife, who gave me the opportunity to test my skills; to the many contact people and individuals at the Graduate School of Business at the University of Chicago, the business and engineering colleges at Arizona State University, Northwest Missouri State University, Samford University, Maricopa County Community College District, and Miami-Dade Community College, without whom I would have been unable to complete my task; to Kathleen Garcia for making sure that the beginning and the end of the monograph make sense; and to my husband, Marv, who works wonders with graphics.

INTRODUCTION

The concept of quality is not foreign to the enterprise we call higher education. In fact, from an international perspective, the term "quality" and the phrase "American higher education" are nearly synonymous. The idea of continuous quality suggests a condition of quality over time. By inference then, continuous quality is not a new notion that suddenly burst on the education scene. So, why the current flurry to improve something, namely higher education in America, that has in the past proven to be the very epitome of continuous quality? Why the perception that we have somehow gone awry?

Several reasons come to mind. First, higher education's past successes are now coming back to haunt it. A more sophisticated, better-educated general populace has learned (largely at colleges and universities) to be more discerning—to question and to scrutinize more closely the education process. They hold higher expectations about what kind of education their sons and daughters and they, themselves, should receive, and they believe they know what effective education programs should look like. Today's learners willingly demand that higher education institutions meet their expectations.

Second, everything we know about learning styles suggests that the changing demographics of America's society in general and its higher education student population in particular will have (and even has today) an immense impact on the way in which we teach future students. Not only will society's complexion change ethnically and racially, but the age range of those attending colleges and universities will expand. On the one hand, the move toward awarding high school diplomas based on competencies instead of seat-time will potentially increase the number of 15- and 16-year-old students attending college. On the other, the general graying of the population will produce a new category of lifelong learners—retirees with time to spare, energy to burn, and an eagerness to rediscover who they are (Kerr, Gade, and Kawaoka 1994).

Third, the exponential expansion of knowledge and the ever-accelerating advances in technology, especially information delivery systems, emphasize the continuous nature of education and signal that teaching the process of learning may be as important as teaching specific course content. Fourth, a growing perception that society must deal with other, more pressing, public needs siphons public (and private) funding away from higher education. For instance, rising health care costs eat away at state and federal appropriations to higher education and at any discretionary income that individuals could, in the past, devote to higher education. Becoming more efficient by containing costs and making more effective use of available resources are familiar scenarios at present-day colleges and universities (Freed, Klugman, and Fife 1994; Layzell, Lovell, and Gill 1994).

Finally, late in this century, the economic importance of education has moved from a personal plane, where an individual's investment in education might improve his or her employability, to a societal level, where the nation's ability to keep pace with and compete in a global economy rests on the education of its work force. To raise the platform for the discussion of education's worth, and ultimately its quality, to such an all-encompassing arena necessarily draws more attention to what colleges and universities do. Most likely, it is this public response to higher education's perceived link to the nation's economic well-being that pushed colleges and universities across the country into the murky waters of continuous quality improvement.

Indeed, some of higher education's most vocal adversarial advocates—American industrial giants like Motorola, AT&T, and Xerox—began pressuring colleges and universities to function more like businesses—to adopt quality principles and techniques and to help produce a work force that they deemed readily employable. The incentive these giants offered was subtle. They voiced a reluctance to continue hiring graduates who had not, during their college or university experiences, acquired skills and competencies conducive to quality management (Coate 1992).

Unaccustomed to such public scrutiny but very much aware that times had changed, that money was no longer as plentiful as it had been in the past, and that, ultimately, the public, not the university, controlled the purse strings, administrators saw merit in learning how to do more with less. The obvious place to begin was operations, but the profound changes that industry and government began to spell out dealt, not with what happened in the president's office, but with what took place in the classroom. Few colleges and universities have addressed this arena. Most of these efforts are fairly recent, rely on individual faculty initiative, and consequently struggle because they lack coordination. Many remain halfhearted exercises, which reluctant faculty wish would simply go away.

The purpose of this monograph is to describe several colleges and universities (or units within the university) that decided upon a more proactive and systemic approach to changing the way faculty function in their classrooms and what they teach. The following subsection introduces the reader to a brief overview of five primary business and educational perspectives on continuous quality improvement—those of Deming, Juran, Crosby, Cornesky, and Seymour. Although the vocabulary varies with the targeted audience (manufacturers, service providers, educators), all share a common origin in statistical quality control and its offspring, total quality management (TQM). Deming and Juran wrote essentially for a manufacturing audience, Crosby for the service industry, particularly the retail sector. Cornesky and Seymour began the translation to higher education. Much can be gained from an understanding of the vernacular transition that took place as the concepts moved from the world of manufacturing into the retail arena and finally into higher education. Therefore, at the risk of inducing an element of terminology trepidation in readers, the nomenclature used is allowed to evolve over the course of the discussion.

The purpose of this monograph is to describe . . . a more proactive and systemic approach to changing the way faculty function in their classrooms and what they teach.

TQM: Its Origins in Organizations of Mass Production
Following the post–World War II collapse of its economic infrastructure, Japan began the process of rebuilding. But poor quality and inefficiency plagued industry and threatened its eminent demise. Faced with crises that it could no longer ignore, Japan's business community proved to be a fertile ground for the ideas of two American consultants, W. E. Deming and J. M. Juran, and their approaches to doing business. Instead of manufacturing products and then inspecting the completed products for flaws, Deming and Juran challenged businesses to inspect the way their products were produced and eliminate any flaw-producing mechanisms that lay within the manufacturing processes. By doing so, they would build good quality into the product instead of inspecting bad quality out of the product.

Deming
Deming arrived on the Japanese scene in 1951. Firmly grounded in statistical quality control, his approach to quality represented a radical departure from traditionally rational

views of organizational management, which laid the blame for inefficiency and poor quality at the feet of the employees.

To Deming, lack of quality results from ineffective management of the processes used to produce a firm's products. Traditionally, management defined these processes within the confines of the organization. Deming insisted that who provides a firm's materials (its suppliers), who purchases its products (its customers), who finances its operations (its investors), and the community in which it resides all impact and are a part of the organization's processes. He accused management of trying to dictate too finely how individual employees carry out work-related tasks. This misdirected control, according to Deming, leads to unrealistic expectations and misplaced responsibility for both the workers and the process (Gitlow and Gitlow 1987, p. 8; Pall 1987).

To Deming's mind, viewing organizations as extended processes demands a new philosophy of management based on strategic thinking that allows for better coordination of activities and greater consistency across processes over time. He summarized his thoughts in a 14-point program to which firms must steadfastly adhere. Among these directives, he called upon businesses to not only meet today's needs but also to plan for the future by becoming competitive, staying in business, and focusing on the well-being of their employees. Deming referred to this concept as "constancy of purpose." He stressed that managers must adopt a new philosophy and take on leadership for change in a new global economy. He chided business for its belief that quality inspection is the last step of the manufacturing process instead of an integral part of each phase of the process. He warned that relying on the lowest price to determine which suppliers a firm used would not necessarily guarantee quality inputs to its manufacturing processes. He suggested, however, that building ongoing relationships based on trust and loyalty would (Deming 1982; Pall 1987).

Under the Deming scenario, continuous improvement is the only true route to improved quality, greater productivity (less rework and perhaps more efficient work routines), and reduced cost. To him, costs of failure, like repair expenditures and customer ill-will, far outweigh costs of prevention, for instance, process design, change, and maintenance. Leaders must advocate on-the-job training to keep employees' skills current and drive out fear because it discourages risk taking and stifles creativity. They must break down departmental barriers that prohibit cross-functional teamwork, because work, by its very nature, does not always recognize such artificial boundaries. He recommended the elimination of productivity slogans, exhortations, and quotas. He believed that pressing for zero defects or new levels of productivity, for example, implies that the employee is at fault, when in reality, the bulk of the causes of poor quality and low productivity belongs to the system and exists in spite of the work force. By the same token, he suggested that quotas do nothing more than perpetuate the status quo and that managing without knowledge of what to do only creates instability and causes fear. Deming believed that people need to take pride in what they do. To keep pace with industry changes and actively contribute to the organization's future, he encouraged education, professional development, and personal self-improvement for everyone. He proclaimed that organizational transformation is everybody's job—that, in effect, top management has to accept the responsibility for continuous quality improvement and provide a financial and philosophical structure that provides employees with the tools and incentives for engaging in change (Deming 1982; Gitlow and Gitlow 1987).

Juran

Underlying Juran's quality philosophy is the belief that the product or service provided should do what the user wants, needs, and expects it to do—that a certain "fitness of use" exists (Schuler and Harris 1992). According to Juran, only 20 percent of all quality problems encountered by an organization are employee controllable (motivation and dedication, for instance). Like Deming, he believes that all other quality problems lie beyond the control of individual employees and are therefore controllable only by management. These quality problems might include failure to improve product design, failure to introduce new products, and failure to make new technology available to the work force. Juran stresses the importance of leadership by upper management, company-wide training of management, and the use of three basic quality-oriented processes—planning, control, and improvement. He focuses on chronic problems, which represent long-standing adverse situations. He advocates employee empowerment by providing the employee with knowledge about what is expected, what the standards for design, output, and operations are, and how to correct any unacceptable variance from standards. He suggests that by doing so, firms can achieve quality "breakthroughs," which lead to higher levels of organizational performance (Juran 1964; Pall 1987).

His tools and methods support improvement of product quality along five dimensions—design, conformance, availability, safety, and field use. Interdisciplinary cooperation determines product design specifications; conformance ensures that the finished product reflects the intended design. Availability suggests that a problem-free product results from careful processing steps, close relations with vendors and customers, and continual feedback on ways to address quality. Safety and field use both focus on concerns of customers, such as product delivery, field-service competence, timeliness, and product risk to the consumer. Juran weaves these quality dimensions together through a system of accountability that centers on the cost of poor quality (rework and customer dissatisfaction)—costs that can be eliminated if organizations concentrate on quality management (Schuler and Harris 1992).

Broadening the Perspective: Philip Crosby

Twenty-five years later, Philip Crosby moved the Deming-Juran quality philosophy beyond the engineer's perspective and into the service industry. Crosby bases his 14-step continuous quality improvement program on four absolutes: the definition of quality is conformance to requirements (meeting acceptable standards); the only acceptable performance standard is zero defects; defect prevention (doing the right thing the first time instead of relying on inspection to eliminate defective products) is the management system of quality; and the cost of quality is the price of nonconformance (what it costs when we do things wrong). The cost of quality is associated solely with defects—making, finding, repairing, or avoiding them (Crosby 1979, 1984; Kennedy 1991; Pall 1987).

Crosby's total belief in a zero-defect goal differs slightly from Juran's. While Juran focuses on appraisal and prevention costs, he contends that these costs may outweigh the costs of poor quality. To him, the goal must be the highest quality at the lowest cost. An organization must pursue assessment and prevention activities to the point at which they equal the cost of poor quality. Beyond that point, Juran questions the desirability of zero defects (Schuler and Harris 1992).

Crosby differs from Deming not so much in content as in degree. While both see quality improvement as ongoing, Deming seeks to eliminate abnormal or special statistical variances and to reduce the level of those inherent to the system. Deming terms this second type of variance "common." Unlike an employee who makes a product but has little direct contact with the product's consumer, service employees interact on a personal level with clients. Customer dissatisfaction caused by poor quality may result in the disappearance of the customer and rob the service provider of the opportunity to remove imperfections. Consequently, a commitment to quality, as Crosby sees it, means "doing it right the first time." Like Deming, Crosby views eliminating variance as important, but he takes a less quantifiable tack than Deming. His strategy calls for quality councils among employees, administrators, and clients that strive for zero defects upon delivery (Crosby 1979; Deming 1982).

The Baldrige Criteria: Drawing the Basic Elements Together

Thirty years after its introduction in Japan, American businesses, such as Xerox, Hewlett-Packard, the Ford Motor Company, and Motorola, began to realize the potential of TQM. Today, new books and articles on the subject of quality management arrive almost daily, and while the views of Deming, Juran, and Crosby represent a relatively small sampling of current quality management gurus, they are considered by most to be the preeminent writers in the quality movement (Peters and Waterman 1982; Stewart 1992).

The American business community, unlike Japan, has been slow to recognize the need for quality initiatives and consequently has, until recently, paid these writers little heed. Lulled into complacency by postwar prosperity, American industry mistakenly identified gradual declines in revenues generated and market share gained or maintained as temporary glitches in the business cycle. To complicate matters further, punitive motivational systems reinforced managerial control and perpetuated a truncated perception of organizational quality and responsibility.

Those firms willing to ask hard questions about productivity, profitability, and quality soon discovered nothing temporary about the downward spiral that they had entered, which dampened competitiveness and threatened to permanently cripple them. A crisis, while perhaps not here, was certainly impending. To encourage American firms to pay serious attention to quality, Congress in 1987 passed legislation that established the annual Malcolm Baldrige National Quality Award. The seven criteria (listed below) set forth by Congress mirror certain common elements of the three approaches already discussed and provide a synthesis of the crucial points made by Deming, Juran, and Crosby.

Leadership: *Facilitation and guidance are key elements of this criterion. Personal leadership from senior executives that helps create and sustain a customer focus must be based on clear and visible quality values.*

Information and Analysis: *Under the specifications of this criterion, timeliness, reliability, access, and the way in which information is analyzed suggest the degree to which data inform organizational decisions and overall operational and planning objectives. The effective employment of adequate information in the organization's problem-solving process must support a firm's drive for quality and its attempts to improve performance.*

Strategic Quality Planning: *This category reinforces the notion that strategic planning encompasses setting short- and long-term goals, developing plans to realize these goals, and implementing their prescribed actions. All key quality requirements must be integrated into the planning process and clearly visible in the plan's deployment across all work units.*

Human Resource Development and Management: *Here examiners look for organizational devotion to employee development and [leadership's] determination to manage this most valuable resource by creating a work environment that supports personal empowerment, shared responsibility, and innovative and ongoing quality improvement.*

Management of Process Quality: *Behind this Baldrige requirement lies the belief that more can be accomplished by working together to improve the system than by having individual contributors working around the system. The key elements of process management include design, production, delivery, support, and assessment. Systematic quality improvement not only includes the efforts of all work units but those of the suppliers of the product or service's various components. Contributors include all work units and suppliers. The system refers to stages of design, production, delivery, support, and assessment.*

Quality and Operational Results: *The supposition that forms the rationale for this category is that improving quality ultimately leads to improved productivity. Results are assessed by comparing organizational quality levels to those of competitors and current industrial benchmarks.*

Customer Focus and Satisfaction: *Of the seven categories, customer focus and satisfaction carries the most weight. It refers to the firm's relationships with customers and its knowledge of its customers' present and anticipated requirements and of the key quality factors that determine marketplace competitiveness.*

Complementing these seven criteria is the solid conviction that "the concept of quality improvement is directly applicable to small companies as well as large, to service industries as well as manufacturing, and to the public as well as private sector enterprise" (Rio Salado Community College 1991b, pp. 10–24; U.S. Department of Commerce 1992, pp. 13–35).

TQM: Its Movement into Higher Education
Education's interest in total quality management lagged that of American business, but by the mid-1980s academic writers and some universities and colleges saw the inherent limitations in the dominant planning routines of the day and began experimenting with strategic management. Existing variations on the theme, such as logical incrementalism, strategic planning, strategic management, strategic issues management, and strategic negotiation, were also revived and expanded (see Ansoff 1980; Cope 1987; Fisher and Ury 1981; Keller 1983; and Quinn 1980 for discussions of these approaches).

Strategic management has much in common with total quality management. It emphasizes an ongoing process that inte-

grates strategic planning with other management systems. Ultimately, it strives to provide the organization with the capacity
for mastering the events and consequences of rapid environmental change. Strategic management encompasses both the
formulation and implementation of strategic plans. Under strategic management, the organization systematically trains its
members to exhibit behaviors that support any new organizational values and to reinforce the new vision. This managerial mentality, which equates employee conditioning to organizational buy-in, reinforces strategic management's predom-
inately top-down approach to planning (Dooris and Lozier
1990; Koteen 1989).

Chaffee moves the academic discussion beyond strategic
management when she begins her discourse on linear, adaptive, and interpretive strategies. She suggests that, while linear
strategies like strategic planning may succeed in insulating
an organization from its environment (as long as that environment remains predictable), the same cannot be said of
it when times become turbulent. Adaptive and interpretive
strategies, in contrast, concentrate on constituent perceptions
of the organization and stress taking action to maximize positive perceptions and repair negative ones by matching organizational activities to environmental demands. Even though
Chaffee stresses constituent satisfaction, cooperation, and
open communication as she moves her discussion into the
arena of total quality management, her arguments exhibit the
same central weakness that characterizes prior academic
approaches to planning. No one questions the underlying
assumption that quality exists and that it exists at an acceptable level (Chaffee 1989; Chaffee and Sherr 1992).

Altering the Concepts: TQM in Academic Terms
Although pioneering institutions of higher education, such
as Fox Valley Technical College and Delaware County Community College, began experimenting with Crosby's model
of quality management as early as 1986, most academic writings and efforts to institutionalize quality management in colleges and universities have occurred since 1990. Discussions
began in earnest with publication of *Using Deming to Improve
Colleges and Universities* by Robert Cornesky et al. in 1990
and *On Q: Causing Quality in Higher Education* by Daniel
Seymour in 1992.

Cornesky: The Deming way

In his first writings, Cornesky simply reframes Deming's 14 points in academic terms. The prescriptive nature of *Using Deming* basically illustrates for colleges and universities how they might integrate Deming's philosophy into institutions of higher education. Cornesky's academic variations of Deming's principles include:

1. Achieve constancy of purpose (i.e., involve both faculty and administrators in long-range planning).
2. Adopt a new philosophy. This means incorporate quality into the administrative system.
3. Cease dependence on inspection. The suggestion is to establish a system of random course testing by outside evaluators because routine testing does not necessarily indicate quality.
4. Build long-term relationships with the school districts and community colleges of potential students and with suppliers.
5. Improve constantly. Cornesky ties this point to the way in which funds are allocated and concludes that funding alone will not guarantee quality.
6. Institute on-the-job training for academic affairs employees and coordinate it with training efforts in other departments.
7. Institute leadership. Cornesky defines effective leadership in terms of planning, performance expectations, and innovation and proposes four strategies—attend to vision, create meaning through communication, build trust through posturing, and instill confidence through respect.
8. Drive out fear. In this case, Cornesky suggests using a Deming technique—the fishbone chart—to elicit candid responses to problems. He spends considerable time discussing conflict management techniques and relates point 8 back to point 7.
9. Break down barriers by letting faculty, students, and staff have their say. Cornesky's examples in this instance are curious—involvement in raising funds and pooling resources across departments.
10. Eliminate slogans, because in many cases the end result is an adversarial relationship.
11. Eliminate quotas. Here Cornesky harkens back to resource allocation and suggests that funding formulas should not

be the sole determinants of personnel and budget distribution.

12. Abolish annual ratings. Cornesky believes that they create barriers to pride in workmanship. Instead, student evaluation of instruction and the course, faculty evaluation of the students and the course, self-evaluations and peer evaluations should constitute new instructor evaluation procedures.

13. Use education and self-improvement on a continual basis to bring about constant improvement. Cornesky refers back to the need to involve educators in planning because, although administrators control the resources, faculty know the problems.

14. Get everyone involved, especially on an interdepartmental basis. To Cornesky, everyone needs to see the big picture.

In his elaboration of these points, Cornesky uses examples of current practice, many of which violate one or more of Deming's points, to illustrate selected points. Where neither good nor bad instances of practice exist, he creates hypothetical scenarios (Cornesky et al. 1990).

In subsequent work, Cornesky elaborates on Crosby's 14 points, provides a guide to TQM tools and techniques, and develops a quality index based on the seven Baldrige criteria (see Cornesky 1993, 1994; Cornesky and McCool 1992; Cornesky et al. 1991). To him, there are five critical conditions that must be met sequentially to implement TQM in an academic setting—education and administrative commitment, education and commitment of faculty and staff, trust, pride in workmanship, and cultural change in the institution (Cornesky et al. 1991).

Seymour: Strategic quality management
Seymour takes a slightly different tack. Rather than superimpose any one style of industrial quality management on higher education, he begins by defining quality and proceeds to the development of his own version of TQM—strategic quality management. Seymour grounds his definition of quality in the work of David Garvin. Garvin, in turn, based his interpretation of quality on insights gained from Deming, Juran, and Crosby (Garvin 1992, cited in Schuler and Harris 1992, p. 20).

Both Juran and Crosby define quality through the eyes of the producer—"fitness of use" in the first case and "conformance to requirements" in the latter. Deming sees quality as mutually determined by those who produce the product and those who consume it. Garvin expanded these perspectives into eight dimensions of quality—performance, features, reliability, conformance, durability, serviceability, aesthetics, and perceptions of quality. Using these dimensions, he derives five definitions of quality—transcendent or innate excellence; manufacturing-based, which relates to Crosby's conformance to requirements; product-based, which is precise and measurable; value-based, which takes Juran's cost-effectiveness into account; and user-based, or the satisfaction of consumer wants (Crosby 1979; Garvin 1992; Juran 1964; Schuler and Harris 1992) .

Use education and self-improvement on a continual basis to bring about constant improvement.

While traditionalists build reputational quality (Garvin's transcendent quality), Seymour suggests that higher education today can ill afford such a narrow interpretation. He instead embraces Garvin's definitional multiplicity. His approach to quality is one of continuous improvement. He sees leadership commitment as the key determinant of whether a college or university succeeds in creating what he terms a culture of quality. He places added emphasis on communication.*

A continuous thread throughout his book deals with customer satisfaction and meeting consumer demands. By focusing on students as customers, he stresses the importance of the interface between the educator and the customer more than Cornesky does. This preoccupation with the concept of customer may stem from his familiarity with the Baldrige criteria and the heavy emphasis that the award places on customer service. Seymour describes institutions of higher education that are devoted to quality as learning organizations that possess "cultures of quality," yet he suggests that the way to change organizations to meet the demands of their customers lies in "managing in quality." In effect, strategic quality management is something done to, and not necessarily by, an organization (Seymour 1991, 1992).

In later work, Seymour softens his rhetoric and relies more and more on Baldrige criteria when he describes quality, quality management, and continuous quality improvement (Seymour 1994). He concludes *TQM: A Critical Assessment* by say-

---

*Seymour mistakenly comments that Deming does not address the need for communication. But Deming defines his first point—constancy of purpose—in terms of commitment to and communication of a vision by organizational leaders. Deming again suggests the need for strong communication when he discusses how to break down organizational barriers.

ing, "In our classrooms we encourage students to examine competing theories, test assumptions, create learning situations. . . . Perhaps this is the time to apply what we teach to what we do."

The Baldrige Criteria for Higher Education

In 1995, the U.S. Department of Commerce launched the Malcolm Baldrige National Quality Award Education Pilot. Through the pilot, the department hopes to determine the viability of a nationwide recognition program, to evaluate the pilot criteria, and to determine what potential an educational Baldrige program might hold for promoting information sharing, cross-sector cooperation, and more demanding education standards. Participation is open to all public and private for-profit and nonprofit U.S. schools and postsecondary institutions (U.S. Department of Commerce 1995a, 1995b, 1995c).

The education pilot builds on the same seven-part framework that the business award uses. In effect, pilot documents to some degree bridge the gap between business jargon and educational lingo. The primary focus is on learning-centered education that pays attention to the needs of learners as dictated by the requirements of the marketplace and the responsibility of citizenship. As learning-centered organizations, institutions serve as role models both operationally and through support of publicly important purposes such as environmental excellence and community service. Active learning, the need for internal networking across units, and the necessity of external partnering with businesses, other education institutions, the community, and service organizations provide cornerstones for the pilot's criteria (U.S. Department of Commerce 1995a, 1995b, 1995c).

Excellence is defined in terms of value-added performance. Internally, this means year-to-year improvement; externally, it implies improvement compared to peer institutions and appropriate benchmarks. Considerable emphasis is placed on cause-effect thinking, but a disclaimer states that "no presupposition of mechanistic models of student development" exists nor is there any need to "document procedures or define conformity or compliance." The seven Baldrige education pilot criteria can be summarized as follows:

Leadership *must be student-centered, focus on clear goals, and hold high expectations. It must ensure the integration of these objectives into the entire management system.*

Information and Analysis *must support overall mission-related performance excellence. This includes benchmarking and peer comparisons.*

Strategic Quality and Operational Planning *must be carried out in terms of key student and overall institutional performance requirements.*

Human Resource Development and Management *includes the examination of faculty and staff professional development to judge whether these efforts align with institutional performance objectives and employee well-being and satisfaction to gain a sense of whether the institution's climate is conducive to performance excellence. Institutions must determine how faculty organize themselves for work and how reward and evaluation systems support a student focus.*

Educational and Business Process Management *is responsible for learning-centered educational design and delivery, support and service design, and business operations. It requires that the organization examine its contributions to the body of knowledge (research), to knowledge transfer (scholarship), and to service.*

Student Performance Results, *as a category, looks at student performance, institutional education climate improvement, organizational business performance, and research and scholarship results. It requires the presence of embedded, ongoing assessment that is both curriculum-based and criterion-referenced.*

Student Focus and Student and Stakeholder Satisfaction *refers to an organization's ability to assess student needs and expectations and to provide effective linkages to other key stakeholders. This category and* Student Performance Results *carry equal weight and together account for nearly one-half the total possible points in the criteria rating system* (Cornesky 1995; U.S. Department of Commerce 1995a, 1995b, 1995c).

The Barriers to CQI in Higher Education
Although the academic community has entered the CQI dialogue, organizational characteristics, perceived to be unique

by educators, complicate the subject's deliberation. When we take a hard look at both academic and business literature, however, certain parallels begin to emerge, all of which seem to point to problems of practice rather than to the incompatibility of the concept.

A lack of forethought, a misinterpretation of quality, and a liquidity of commitment

Caught in the tangled web of today's problems, organizations often enter into a frenzy of activity with no clear idea of what lies ahead. They leave intact generic mission statements, which make defining quality and excellence impossible. These institutions practice short-run leadership intervention instead of connecting daily operational decision making with some form of long-term planning (Deming 1982; Ewell 1993).

Enticed by the prospect of minimal organizational disruption and turmoil and the promise of organizational transformation, they succumb to the lure of gadgetry, new technology, and slick-sounding problem-solving techniques commonly associated with off-the-shelf CQI programs. In higher education, drawn-out debates about the relevance of Deming's 14 points and skepticism of core academic units, because their members see CQI as unrelated to their concerns, generate resistance to such ill-conceived approaches. Furthermore, disciplinary loyalty rather than institutional affiliation prevents cross-functional teams, which would link planning with operational processes, from materializing. This breeds a separatism that shelters strategic planning efforts from integration with total quality management and solidifies a continued disconnection between institutional goals and individual goals (Ewell 1993; Seymour 1992; Teeter and Lozier 1993).

Using worn-out techniques to teach old dogs new tricks

Instead of moving toward long-term change, organizations often equate CQI to a short-term quick fix. In both business and education, a desperate search for instant success disallows the opportunity to commit to an all-encompassing endeavor like quality improvement. In their enthusiasm to "get the show on the road," organizations either attempt large-scale, diffuse implementation or engage in massive training programs. In the first instance, organizations devote too little time and too few people to extremely complex projects. In the latter, they tend to use programs that are prepackaged and unable to focus on the organization's particular needs. Heavy concentration on tools and process improvement subverts any possible conveyance of overall strategy and purpose. The final flaw is that instead of having too few people trained, too many are too willing to practice something for which too few opportunities exist (Seymour 1992; Teeter and Lozier 1993).

Ritualistic commitment to tools that lead to measuring for the sake of measuring
Organizations are what they measure, but what gets measured may not give them the information they really need to know. As measuring becomes an end in itself, too much data pile up and sheer volume often leads to faulty analysis. Misplaced benchmarks become targets instead of guides and fail to reflect accurate institutional and specific functional definitions of quality and excellence (Ewell 1993; Matthews 1993; Seymour 1992; Teeter and Lozier 1993).

A lack of urgency and a myopic perspective on expertise and quality applicability
Where no perceived catastrophe exists, no sense of urgency emerges and a general aversion to change perpetuates inaction. This lack of urgency currently permeates much of America's service industry sector, a good portion of its manufacturing sector, and almost all of its institutions of higher education. Further complications arise when organizations believe that they know best how to solve their own problems. The paradox here is that they contribute to their present dilemmas by continuing to use the time-worn strategies that led to their problems in the first place. Organizations assume that quality exists, so discussions of quality management seem irrelevant and business as usual precludes the recognition of telltale signs that signal a need for change (Seymour 1992; Waterman 1987).

Choosing the wrong issues
Deming says organizations that claim their troubles lie entirely in the workforce miss the mark. The consequence of such thinking is a business run on the basis of visible figures alone. By counting money and insisting on improvement based on production quotas, these organizations fail to realize that workers are handicapped by organizational systems over which they have little control. In other words, quality and

quality improvement may depend on systemic changes, which fall within the realm of managerial rather than employee influence.

In the case of higher education, the faculty-controlled teaching and learning process lies at the heart of every college and university. By confining quality change efforts to administrative practices and academic support services, we may be missing opportunities to make significant inroads in the search for quality education.

Segregating rather than integrating quality improvement

Businesses and colleges and universities alike tend to embrace quality as an add-on. They invest quality control departments with the responsibility for taking care of problems of quality. By doing so, they in effect divorce quality from the mainstream of institutional life (Deming 1982).

Clinging to outmoded reward structures

Deming insists that most performance evaluations, merit ratings, and annual reviews focus on an end product and do not promote leadership that helps people improve. In fact, merit systems can rapidly degenerate into number counting games. Most do not take team effort into account. In education, improperly focused systems discourage quality creativity, promote business as usual, and, coupled with tenure, spawn the attitude that quality and excellence are highly laudable concepts as long as someone else has to worry about them (Deming 1982; Matthews 1993; Teeter and Lozier 1993).

High-level lip service, linear views of change, and inattention to cultural transformation

Leaders show a reluctance to play an aggressive and creative role in institutional moves toward quality. They see no connection between quality and the real problems that their organizations face. Politicized turfmanship instead of teamwork emerges among middle-level managers (in education— department chairs) who, because they may have been left out of the planning process, do not understand or welcome new roles. A continued short-term perspective denies the need for an extended time frame. Leaders who focus on operational costs and budgets overlook the immediate costs in money and time required to make CQI routine. This bottom-line mentality and an accompanying dependence on decision making by decree discourage consensus building, which is a basic prerequisite to cultural transformation. Paradoxically, leaders who successfully expand participation through planning may also increase the level and the extent of constituency frustration (Deming 1982; Matthews 1993; Poulton 1980; Seymour 1993; Teeter and Lozier 1993).

One sticky issue: The customer image
The term "customer" sparks indignation not only in educators but in many industrial and service organizations as well. For years, American businesses have followed Say's Law—supply creates demand. In other words, the customer indiscriminately settles for whatever business chooses to offer. Educators reject the notion of customer out of hand. To most, such a connection implies blind submission to someone's (most likely a student's) unfettered demands. The problem with this aversion to the student-as-customer image is the potential for misinterpretation of learning needs.

Matthews suggests that when educators do not determine the goals and desires of their primary stakeholders (students and sources of financial support), they substitute those of education's secondary stakeholders—administrators and faculty. Even the goals of third-level stakeholders—boards, cities, future employees—many times take primacy over the needs of students (Matthews 1993). Ewell contends that this does not have to be the case. Instead, the key to pleasing education's customers lies in the total quality concept of actively shaping customer reactions by anticipating and exceeding current expectations (Ewell 1993). To Seymour, the student-as-customer frame of reference poses the greatest hurdle for advocates of CQI in higher education. He sums up the problem by saying, "As students, they belong to us; as customers, the learning process is mutually owned" (Seymour 1993).

Prelude to the Case Studies
What follows next are case studies of seven educational organizations (two at the same university) and their attempts to move in a fairly substantive way beyond exposure to TQM in their administrative superstructures to continuous quality in the classroom. With varying degrees of success, each has tried to avoid the numerous pitfalls of practice in its efforts to institutionalize CQI.

The organizations include the Graduate School of Business at the University of Chicago, the Colleges of Business and Engineering at Arizona State University (ASU), Northwest Missouri State University (NWMSU), Samford University, the Maricopa County Community College District (MCCCD), and Miami-Dade Community College (MDCC). Several considerations weighed heavily in choosing these institutions. First, the desire was to provide a broad range of organizations in terms of size, location, and institutional type. Two colleges are located in the Southwest, two in the Midwest, and two in the Southeast. Most are situated in urban areas with more than 2 million residents; only NWMSU, in rural Missouri, and Samford, in Birmingham, Alabama, serve fewer people. ASU and the University of Chicago are large research universities, NWMSU and Samford University are comprehensive four-year institutions, and Maricopa and Miami-Dade are community colleges. Four of the colleges receive public funding; two exist as private, independent institutions. The two community colleges serve more than 50,000 students, both the engineering college and the business college at ASU enroll between 5,000 and 8,000 students, and the others range in size from 1,500 to slightly over 6,000 enrollees.

Second, past publicity about CQI efforts played a role. An attempt was made to introduce several institutions, among them ASU's Colleges of Business and Engineering and the University of Chicago's Graduate School of Business, that up to this point have received little or no comprehensive coverage. These colleges complement three others—Northwest Missouri State University, Samford University, and the Maricopa County Community College District—that have garnered extensive attention. The final case illustrates how the discussion of continuous quality might be broadened. It details quality initiatives at a community college that does not regard itself as a CQI institution. Miami-Dade embraces neither the CQI dialogue, its methods, nor its jargon, yet its faculty pursue many of the avenues traveled by CQI educational organizations. In many instances, Miami-Dade Community College does so more wholeheartedly and effectively than colleges and universities that operate under the banner of CQI.

Information for the case studies came from internal documents, published materials, and interviews.

THE CASE STUDIES

The case studies in this section focus on seven educational organizations (two at the same university) and their attempts to move from exposure to TQM in the administrative superstructure to continuous quality in the classroom. With varying degrees of success, each has tried to institutionalize continuous quality improvement.

Several considerations weighed heavily in choosing these institutions, among them the desire to provide a broad range of organizations in terms of size, location, and institutional type. Two colleges are located in the Southwest, two in the Midwest, and two in the Southeast. Most are located in urban areas with more than 2 million residents; only NWMSU, in rural Missouri, and Samford, in Birmingham, Alabama, serve fewer people. ASU and the University of Chicago are large research universities, NWMSU and Samford University are comprehensive four-year institutions, and Maricopa and Miami-Dade are community colleges. Four of the colleges receive public funding; two are private, independent institutions. They serve from 1,500 to more than 50,000 students.

Second, past publicity about CQI efforts played a role. An attempt was made to introduce several institutions, among them ASU's Colleges of Business and Engineering and the University of Chicago's Graduate School of Business, that up to this point have received little or no comprehensive coverage. These colleges complement three others—NWMSU, Samford, and the Maricopa County Community College District—that have garnered extensive attention.

The final case illustrates how the discussion of continuous quality might be broadened. It details quality initiatives at a community college that does not regard itself as a CQI institution. Miami-Dade embraces neither the CQI dialogue, its methods, nor its jargon, yet its faculty pursue many of the avenues traveled by CQI educational organizations. In many instances, Miami-Dade does so more wholeheartedly and effectively than colleges and universities that operate under the banner of CQI.

Information for the case studies came from internal documents and published materials. In addition, because the author had ready access to people at Arizona State University, the Maricopa County Community College District, and Miami-Dade Community College, interview data supplement written sources. Few of the colleges use the same nomenclature to

The case studies in this section focus on . . . attempts to move from exposure to TQM in the administrative superstructure to continuous quality in the classroom.

describe their efforts. Because the labels themselves add richness to each college's individual story, no attempt has been made to standardize terminology across cases.

Grassroots Quality: The University of Chicago Graduate School of Business

The Graduate School of Business at the University of Chicago employs 115 full-time and 34 part-time faculty who serve about 1,100 full-time and 1,300 part-time students. In fall 1988, *Business Week* published a report in which the university's school received low marks in a customer-satisfaction survey of graduating MBA students (Bemowski 1991). The dean of the school, who was heavily involved in fund-raising, could devote little time to a hands-on improvement effort. Instead, he encouraged a series of faculty- and student-inspired endeavors. The grassroots model that emerged has one minimal requisite—the organization must permit substantial freedom to individuals in how they perform their own jobs and how small work groups function (Roberts 1993).

At Chicago, this flexibility existed. Consequently, by 1989, when much of the current grassroots quality initiative began, several pieces already were in place. For example, instructors already prepared up-to-date, detailed course descriptions for a widely disseminated curriculum guide. The use of interactive computing in courses, including the development of educational software, was widespread; student-evaluation results were reported publicly; and several electives in TQM existed. A statistics professor and a professor of management science, for instance, already offered Applied Production and Operations Management, in which students analyze Japanese management techniques. A long-standing course, Quality and Productivity Improvement, emphasizes statistical techniques used in quality-improvement efforts and introduces certain Deming management concepts (Roberts 1993).

Since 1990, visiting "practitioner-scholars" have offered courses that explore quality policy issues, such as those surrounding the Baldrige competition, and familiarize students with the Deming/Shewhart Plan-Do-Check-Act cycle. A seminar in quality, innovation, and competitiveness also was introduced. And students participate in such courses as Design for Manufacturability, which are offered by the Motorola Training and Education Center (Roberts 1990). Currently, the school offers about a dozen electives in quality yearly, and overall, quality ideas have become significant components in several introductory core courses. For example, approximately 35 percent of the core course in operations management is devoted to quality. In 1990, quality management became one of Chicago's basic fields of study and an area for doctoral specialization (Roberts 1993).

LEAD: Uniquely grassroots

One of Chicago's first grassroots undertakings was to gather information. Through surveys and focus groups, the University of Chicago's business school discovered that its students and alumni viewed the MBA program as heavily theoretical, with little attention paid to the acquisition of leadership and human relations skills (Bemowski 1991). As a result, the school recruited a team of first-year MBA students and charged them with developing a special course called Leadership Education and Development, or LEAD.

LEAD is a noncredit course that functions largely independently of the regular curriculum and relies on class members' involvement in both assessment and content revision (Coate 1990). Developed specifically for first-year MBA students by a team of second-year MBA students, it focuses on aspects of business leadership, such as communications, risk taking, negotiations, and ethics, that Chicago faculty believe are difficult to introduce into traditional courses (Zangwill and Roberts 1993). All first-year students work in cohorts of 50 during the first quarter of their academic studies. Each group is assigned a team of four second-year students, who facilitate activities and discussions. A faculty and staff member are assigned to each cohort and participate along with the first-year students (Roberts 1993).

This course, in turn, led to the formation of the Student Continuous Improvement Committee, which studies curriculum, placement, alumni relations, and policy issues, and a schoolwide Suggestion Forum that elicits and acts upon students' suggestions (Bemowski 1991). The college now has a quality office that supports the dozen or more student/staff teams that regularly work on improvement projects in the areas of student and alumni services and carries out a quarterly exit survey of all graduating students. This office also follows up and reports on the more than 250 suggestions that are received each year from students, staff, and faculty (Roberts 1993).

The teaching lab: Another student inspiration

In 1991, based on a recommendation from an MBA student, Business 712, The Laboratory to Achieve Organizational Excellence: Improvement of Teaching, Curriculum, and Research, took form. In this course, faculty experiment with different ways to enhance their teaching skills. They explore how to use TQM principles and tools to improve teaching, curriculum, and research in a laboratory setting. Students, acting as consultants, assist the faculty participants (Bemowski 1991). During its first year, 11 faculty members worked with lab-course students or student teams on the improvement of ongoing courses, a team of five students worked with behavioral science faculty to design a new required course, three students collaborated with marketing faculty on curricular issues, and another student benchmarked the performance of two of the school's most outstanding case teachers (Bateman and Roberts 1993).

The fast-feedback questionnaire: A lesson from the teaching lab

K.P. Cross, an expert in classroom assessment, draws a direct parallel between traditional CQI tools and techniques and those employed in classroom assessment. It is conducted by the classroom teacher and consists of simple periodic collections of data from students to see what learning is occurring so corrective action can be taken during the current semester.

Assessment might take the form of a test but most often involves more intimate student-faculty exchanges, such as minute papers and one-sentence summaries. The first asks what was learned, how important it is, and what remains unclear. The second asks who did what to whom, how, when, where, and why. A student's ability (or lack of it) to answer these questions brings about a redress of the material being taught and/or the methods being used by the teacher (Cross 1992; Cross and Angelo 1988).

Two faculty members provide examples of how their experiences in the teaching lab altered their behavior as instructors and introduced them to the techniques of classroom assessment. They began putting copies of their course syllabi and a short student-background questionnaire into student mail folders before the first class meeting; each synthesized and focused course readings and provided a clear idea of what specific reading should accomplish. And both started using fast-feedback questionnaires.

To their surprise, the information gained from the fast-feedback surveys pointed to problems that previously had gone undetected. In almost every class, students had problems understanding the professor, reading the writing on the board, or seeing the visuals; quite often, students wanted more examples to illustrate abstract concepts. The instructors modified the way they prepare for class, "We analyze the questionnaires and plan appropriate adjustments almost immediately. . . ." To stress the importance of providing students with feedback, they coined the term "two-way fast feedback," a combination of fast-feedback questionnaires for students and fast written responses from the professor (Bateman and Roberts 1993).

The feedback questionnaires developed in the teaching lab vary depending on the type of class and the instructor, but the questions asked typically refer to course content, delivery style, and student preparation. One statistics professor's survey illustrates the idea (see table 1).

As the semester progresses, the form shortens from two pages to one. Certain questions, such as how much did you get out of today's class and what was the muddiest point, remain constant throughout the term, but others change. For example, by the fourth week, the instructor asks his or her students to assess their ability to handle the computing in the course. The final session feedback relates to overall class impressions. Typically, the instructor spends about one hour tabulating and analyzing questionnaire data. Although increasing numbers of faculty use feedback surveys, the practice is by no means universal (Bateman and Roberts 1993).

The personal quality checklist: A faculty initiative
One of Chicago's faculty (see Roberts 1992) has taken the pursuit of quality a step farther. In the past, he required students in his classes to undertake personal-improvement projects. These projects involved relatively elaborate design, data collection, and analysis and typically resulted in very meager progress in personal improvement. Today, the instructor uses a much simpler approach: the personal quality checklist. With it, he illustrates elementary TQM ideas and gives his students practice in using other tools, such as run charts and Pareto

TABLE 1

FAST-FEEDBACK QUESTIONNAIRE FOR BUS. 520,
WEEK _____ , WINTER 19__

1	2	3	4	5
Little		A		A
or		Fair		Great
Nothing		Amount		Deal

Today's Class:

Overall, how much did you get out of today's class?

What was the most important thing you learned?

What was the muddiest point?

What single change by the instructor would have most
improved the class?

Please comment briefly on the helpfulness of the advance
reading assignment for today's class.

Your Preparation for Today's Class:

Overall, how much did you get out of your preparation
for today's class?

What one thing can the instructor do to help you to
improve your future class preparation?

What one thing can you do to help improve your future
class preparation?

Your Progress on Quality Improvement Projects:

(behind schedule, 1; on schedule, 3; ahead of schedule, 5)

Project 1

Project 2

What one thing can the instructor do to help you make better progress on the projects? _____

What one thing can you do to help yourself make better progress on the
projects? _____

General:

Any other feedback about any aspect of the course, including use of computing or topics that you would
like to hear more about? _____

Are you having problems unrelated to this course that the instructor should be aware of? _____

diagrams. The goal is to help students become better students, and to do so the instructor sets an example by keeping his own personal quality checklist.

He defines desirable categories of personal job performance and keeps track of failures to achieve the goals of each category. He terms these failures "defects." A person establishes goals in two broad categories of personal job performance—waste-reducers or time-savers and additional value-adding activities. For example, "on time to meetings and appointments" might be considered a waste-reducer (or time-saver) and "talk to all direct-reports at least once per week" could be construed to be a value-adding activity (see table 2).

TABLE 2

INSTRUCTOR'S PERSONAL QUALITY CHECKLIST: WEEK OF _____

Defect Category	MON	TUE	WED	THU	FRI	SAT	SUN	TOTAL
Late for meeting or appointment								
Search for something misplaced or lost								
Delayed return of phone call or reply to letter								
Put a small task in a "hold pile"								
Failure to discard incoming junk promptly								
Misses a chance to clean up junk in office								
Unnecessary inspection								
Total								

Comments:

Simple graphing of the number of defects per month against the months of the year reveals the progress (or lack thereof) toward meeting the original goals. No refined statistical analysis is needed to detect drops in the numbers. People who use personal quality checklists caution, however, against producing a list containing too many value-adding activities and too few waste-reducers/time-savers. As one of them says, "Time must be saved before new activities can be added." The categories must be doable. As for the reason for keeping track of defects, a believer in the tool's usefulness states, "Only defects point the way to improvement of the underlying processes. . . ."

During his first go-round, the instructor whose checklist appears in table 2 accumulated seven defects—five for a "search for something misplaced or lost" and two for "unnecessary inspection." He decided that the other five categories were largely "operator controllable" and that the mere existence of the list jogged his memory enough to change his habits. The two categories in which flaws turned up exposed problems with his underlying organizational and filing systems and would take longer to correct (Roberts 1992, 1993).

Closing comments

True to its name, the impetus for change through the grassroots model often originates at fundamental levels—the students and the faculty. By its very nature, this approach requires little hands-on participation by top-level administrators, and, because it rests on voluntary faculty commitment, progress is slow. Yet at Chicago, a small but dedicated band of quality champions seems determined to guide the school along its quality journey. One faculty member sums up his feelings about incorporating TQM perspectives into teaching: "For me, the idea of students as customers led to measurable improvement in my own teaching, especially for students who were not doing well. . . . I could no longer shrug off poor student performance by attributing it to poor attitudes or weak preparation; I realized that I am partly responsible, and I must try to be aware of, identify, and correct the problem" (Bemowski 1991).

College of Business at Arizona State University: Getting Serious about Quality

Twenty percent of Arizona State University's 42,000 students enroll in its College of Business, or COB—about 7,000 at the undergraduate level, the rest as graduate students. Twenty-five percent of all university graduates in any given year come from the COB, but available persistence data show high freshman and lower-division transfer attrition rates (86 percent in the former case and 68 percent in the latter). Although Arizona State serves an ethnically diverse region, students of color currently constitute less than 15 percent of the COB's baccalaureate graduates. As recently as 1991, ASU's day MBA program ranked 197 out of 273. By 1994, *U.S. News & World Report* listed the MBA program among the nation's top 50 programs, and the placement rate of daytime MBA graduates stood at 98 percent, more than 30 points above the national average. What made the difference? (COB 1994b, 1994c).

Embracing the total quality approach

During the last few years, efforts to improve the quality of the college's programs at both the undergraduate and graduate levels can be linked to a total quality approach. In fall 1991, the college, under the guidance of the Dean's Council of 100—a group of influential Phoenix-area business executives—entered into a planning process called ASU Business Partners. With a redefined mission and a preliminary vision developed by the dean, the college began to strategically reorient itself to meet the needs of its environment. Using a process designed by the steering committee of the Business Partners (13 high-level business executives, three faculty, and two students), the college collected the data needed to assess its current educational quality relative to that of its peers. Customer surveys and focused interviews targeted four groups: current students, recent graduates, recruiters, and employers.

The information gathered consistently pointed to four weaknesses. Students noted their inability to solve unstructured, real-world problems and to manage people and the business environment. Employers singled out poor skills in written communication and poor student transition into the workplace as their biggest concerns. Task forces, which formed around the undergraduate program, the MBA program, the doctoral program, the Seidman Research Institute, and faculty development, recommended program revisions that addressed these findings. Much of the college's quality plan that resulted from these recommendations conforms to the criteria set forth for Arizona's Pioneer Award, the state's equivalent of the national Baldrige Award. Five themes—globalization, information technology, TQM, diversity, and communication skills—run across all program and quality initiatives (COB 1993a, 1994b).

With a redefined mission and a preliminary vision developed by the dean, the college began to strategically reorient itself to meet the needs of its environment.

Undergraduate preprofessional and professional programs

Comprehensive changes in programs and program delivery have occurred throughout the undergraduate program. Examples in accounting, economics, and new cross-functional requirements typify the range of activities taking place.

Accounting. Arizona State's School of Accountancy took the lead in the college's quality journey by revising its undergraduate curriculum. About one-third of the program revisions impact course content; more than one-half deal directly with pedagogy, format, and delivery. By fall 1992, the school had re-created its preprofessional program and introduced a series of three courses: two three-credit classes and a third one-hour course. Students, individually and in teams, explore feasible approaches to solving accounting problems and then select and defend their plans of action. One-minute papers, which call for short, concise explanations, help faculty discern whether students have a clear understanding of accounting principles as they pertain to real-world situations. For accounting majors, a required one-hour computerized course acquaints students with the day-to-day mechanics of accounting work.

Schoolwide revisions should be completed by 1996, but already upper-division core courses as well as electives depend heavily on computerization. Preliminary results from these curricular revisions are heartening. The drop rate in preprofessional core accounting courses declined from nearly 40 percent to 3 percent. Outcomes from formal testing of ASU's curricular approach in 25 programs across the country also have been very positive (Smith 1994; Wolverton 1995).

Economics. On another front, the economics department began to examine lower-division micro- and macro-principles classes. Access to the college's professional program depends on completion of these courses. Not only has the success rate been low, but minority students typically experience disproportionate failure rates. Faculty believe that increasing the success rate among all students will ultimately improve the diversity of the college. Seven faculty used one of 11 approaches in classes that ranged in size from 51 to 449 students. Pilot treatments included mandatory graded homework, required computer tutorial assignments, targeted review sessions, voluntary group study sessions with a professor or a tutor, and optional study guides, review packets, and computer tutorials (Blakemore 1994; Wolverton 1995).

The experience of one instructor bears closer scrutiny, because she taught the same courses using the same texts in the previous year but without the pilot modifications. In addition, she employed different instructional options in the two microeconomics pilot sections under her supervision.

In one, she administered five homework assignments that students turned in at an economics study lab. The lab was offered at regularly scheduled times ten hours a week, with teams of graduate students and undergraduate majors providing the tutoring service. The homework constituted 20 percent of the students' grades. At first, students only turned in their assignments, but by midsemester, an average of 100 students per week attended the lab sessions. In her second section, the instructor announced at the beginning of the semester that ten pop quizzes would compose 20 percent of each student's grade. The quizzes covered previous lectures and reading assignments, and students were encouraged but not required to attend the study lab. For the most part, these students did not use the lab (Blakemore 1994; Wolverton 1995).

When the instructor compared the grade distribution of the minority students in the two classes (in the section that required homework), the percentage of those receiving a grade of C or better rose 15 points from the previous year. In the section in which pop quizzes had been administered, the percentage of minority students who received a grade of either D, E, or W remained unchanged from the previous year. Overall, the results of more than 2,200 micro- and macro-students indicate that grade distribution increased in students at large as well as in minority students, particularly in sections that required either homework or computer tutorials or offered targeted review sessions (Blakemore 1994; Wolverton 1995).

New requirements. By 1994, the college's undergraduate committee recommended changes in the configuration of the professional program. Revisions included the addition of an administrative communication course as a first-semester requirement, the establishment of a new standing committee (the core committee) to coordinate the upper-division core and to address inconsistencies in the program's noncore electives, the addition of one elective international course to the core requirements, the incorporation of international issues into all core classes, and the creation of two new required classes (Hershauer 1994).

The new required classes merit further examination. Students encounter both new courses in their junior year. The first is an integrative introduction to the college's professional program. A cross-functional faculty team uses business simulations, comprehensive cases, business audits, historical and current readings, and computer-based analysis to expose students to topics such as organizational dynamics, alternative decision-making models, the use of information and statistics in decision making, TQM in service and manufacturing contexts, quality management from a global perspective, and business ethics. In addition, emphasis is placed on diversity, information technology, service quality, and learning organizations. Specially designed exercises link this course to the required communications course.

The second required course provides a practical bridge between student life and employment life. This one-credit class pays attention to more pragmatic aspects of entering the job market. Sessions deal with proper table etiquette, professional appearance, resume preparation, and how to interview with and make presentations to potential employers (Hershauer 1994; Wolverton 1995).

MBA programs

Prior to quality initiatives, the MBA program had little structure. The associate dean for the MBA programs commented, "People couldn't get the courses that they needed; they drifted in and out. . . . There was no sense of community. . . . Today, we've moved from a disconnected series of courses to what we refer to as 'the MBA experience.'"

The day MBA program couples an intensive first-year experience with a flexible second-year framework. A strong team emphasis and a focus on cooperative learning permeate the program. All first-year core courses in the day and evening MBA programs run on a trimester, lockstep schedule that lasts ten weeks, including exams. The day program requires that its students complete 36 credit-hours in the first year.

Evening students complete six classes during an academic year; special summer courses allow them to graduate in two years. Using this system, the college offers 50 percent more courses in any given nine-month period than previously was possible. Faculty often team-teach core courses. It is quite common, for instance, to find a finance professor lecturing in an accounting or an economics class about the interconnectedness of the two disciplines. Students engage in interdisciplinary projects graded by multiple faculty, businesspeople from the community are being integrated into the classroom as evaluators, and CQI is an issue (COB 1993b, 1994a; McPheters 1994; MBA Program Office 1994).

Part of the first-year experience includes leadership training. In the 1993–94 academic year, this curricular activity took place during the 11th week of each of the first two trimesters and was highlighted by guest corporate speakers, simulations, and a two-day team competition (COB 1994d). Based on students' suggestions, the following year the college no longer showcased leadership training as a special event but integrated it into the program as a yearlong, weekly seminar.

The associate dean commented on a further development. "We also found that there is a strong need for more basic leadership skills, like how to run a meeting, how to plan a project, and how to work in a group. It can be as ordinary as which fork to pick up first or when to use electronic mail versus when to write a letter or use the phone. We don't normally include these topics in the curriculum, but it's what Motorola University offers and what Intel teaches its employees. So we're incorporating this material into the weekly leadership seminars."

The college also lends depth to this first-year experience by including seminars on global topics like the political economy of the rain forests, the collapse of the Soviet Union, and Japanese culture presented by faculty from the College of Liberal Arts and Sciences (MBA Program Office 1994). During the first semester of the year, students also participate in a major daylong community service activity. For example, they might renovate a playground for disadvantaged children. Students then become involved in management-consulting projects for nonprofit agencies in the community during the second half of the year (COB 1994d; MBA Program Office 1994).

The second year of the program provides students with a great deal of flexibility. Students select electives within one area—say, marketing or finance—or plan cross-functional course sequences that integrate such topics as internationalization or quality. This student-designed year can include field projects with potential employers, travel to foreign universities, or course work from other ASU colleges. Students may also enroll in courses at other institutions, such as the American Graduate School of International Management in Phoenix or Norway's Oslo Business School. In addition, the college encourages students to participate between their first and second years in a summer internship program (COB 1993a; MBA Program Office 1994).

Continuous quality efforts in the classroom vary from one instructor to the next and according to discipline. To illustrate the extent to which change has traversed the college, examples from three areas—operations and logistics (a subunit of decision and information systems), marketing, and management—not covered in the undergraduate discussion are highlighted here.

Decision and information systems. An instructor in operations and logistics, who also serves as a Baldrige examiner for the annual national business award, takes students through an exercise that approximates Baldrige training. Case studies from past Baldrige competitions provide detailed and realistic subjects for team projects. He observes, "My experience allows me to teach some things other people can't. It lets me do a better job teaching quality" (Smith 1992). This professor begins his class by finding out about his students. "I ask about their background, their reason for taking the course, and what they expect to get out of it. I then see if I can, in any way, adjust what I had planned to better meet the students' expectations and needs." Most short exercises, spot checks for understanding, and the course project require student teamwork. For instance, instead of administering quizzes with narrowly focused questions that require little more than rote memory to answer, the instructor poses a general question to his students, allows them to break into teams and discuss it, and asks them to arrive at a consensual answer. Grades for some of these exercises depend on the thoroughness and precision of the work; in other cases, teams receive credit simply for completing the work. The Baldrige assessment project includes peer evaluation of team members' performance.

Marketing. In marketing, the recipient of two research rewards between 1990 and 1993 also garnered the COB 1993 outstanding graduate teacher award. This professor studies service quality and services marketing and sees a direct correlation between good research and good teaching. By combining lectures, group in-class exercises, guest lecturers, and group field projects, she illustrates "how ideas play out." Because she believes that MBA students must be able to apply theory in practice, she teaches not only theory but emphasizes critical and group skills as well.

The professor continually experiments. "I like to try a lot of little things in class . . . about 10 percent of those I'd never do again." One long-standing technique helps the instructor draw students into class discussions. At the beginning of every semester, she takes individual instant photos of her students. To each photo, she adds information about the students, their work, families, areas of interest, and course expectations. Whenever the professor meets with a class, she has this information with her (Smith 1993a).

Another marketing professor recently concentrated on TQM in one of his marketing classes. He brought chief executive officers from community businesses into the classroom to talk about TQM and customer satisfaction in their companies. Using a question-and-answer format, students probed into the impact of tough economic times on the quality efforts of the represented firms. The instructor also requires his students to find work in a local organization, such as a YMCA, a major home builder, or a manufacturer, and to analyze the quality of the firm's management (Eskes 1992).

Management. One management professor describes himself as a facilitator. His approach to organizational theory blends the collaborative nature of teams with the individualistic challenges of self-leadership. About 50 percent of the class involves team exercises that often focus on what not to do rather than on how to function effectively as a group. In one such exercise, students within groups assume various barrier-producing roles: controller, appeaser, reclusive. By doing so, they experience the effects of these behaviors on team dynamics. In addition, the instructor has each student complete a personal self-improvement project. Several times a semester, he divides students into quality circles to gain group feedback on the course.

Doctoral programs
The associate dean for doctoral programs says, "The goal for this year is to operationalize our part of the strategic plan." The plan's primary objective at the doctoral level is straightforward—graduate students who meet the academy's market demands for high-quality faculty. It proposes that the college limit the number of students it recruits, that it coordinate recruitment efforts across departments, and that it develop a consistent way to move students through the process. To gain baseline information, the college will survey graduates from the previous three years about whether they were prepared to teach the classes they were asked to teach and to

do the level of research that was expected of them once they left ASU (COB 1994b).

The plan also states that while faculty should hone their students' research skills by actively involving them in the research process, they should also help them become effective teachers. Consequently, first-year students take a course in teaching pedagogy, which emphasizes cooperative and active learning, and are assigned teaching responsibilities for at least one year.

Departments also use a combination of training approaches that complement the classwork. In one, faculty members observe students in teaching situations and feed back information on how each might improve. In another, members of the department and the doctoral students who teach meet once a week and discuss the issues they are facing and how they are resolving them. A third common tactic stresses team-based learning for the doctoral participants, as students and also as teachers. The objective is to develop a common approach across the college. As this teacher-training component becomes institutionalized, teaching evaluations, along with research, will become a part of the annual review for continuation in the doctoral programs.

Benchmarking for the future

One associate dean noted, "We say that we want to look like a leading MBA program. That requires that we know what leading MBA programs look like." To do so, ASU scans reports from other schools for information about entry standards, curriculum content, faculty credentials and salaries, graduate placement, and starting salaries for graduates.

In addition, ASU tries to gather data from peer institutions on college-specific priorities. For instance, although minority representation rarely serves as a program benchmark, admitting and retaining a significantly higher proportion of women and minorities than many other major programs are important considerations at ASU (Madden 1992). In fact, ASU's MBA program may serve as a benchmark for peers in this area. More than 40 percent of its fall 1994 entering students were women (up 5 percent from the year before), and 25 percent of the class held minority status (an increase of 14 percent in one year). Doctoral coordinators are contacting their counterparts at peer or better institutions to ascertain the qualities most valued in graduates who apply for faculty positions in order to establish their own benchmarks. Benchmarking at the undergraduate level remains limited because the college has been unable to collect relevant data about peer or better baccalaureate programs (COB 1994b).

Support for change

For sustained quality improvement, fundamentals like faculty reward and development systems, fiscal resources, leadership, and organizational structure need to encourage quality endeavors. To some extent, these crucial building blocks seem to exist or are being developed by the college.

Faculty rewards, incentives, and development. The associate dean for undergraduate education says, "The college is sending out signals that good teaching matters. Faculty can prepare portfolios to highlight their strengths, but student evaluations are the bottom line even when it comes to decisions about tenure and promotion. On the one hand, yes, we reward research, but a good researcher who is a poor teacher will not be rewarded to the same degree as he or she was in the past. On the other, excellent teachers with relatively modest research records will be rewarded." His MBA counterpart added, "I think the faculty are seeing a little bit of this kind of change, but we have a way to go." Although merit pay seems to be allotted based upon teaching expertise, evidence to substantiate whether the college follows through in its pledge to grant tenure using similar criteria may take time to manifest itself (Wolverton 1995).

Monetary incentives in the form of teaching and travel grants and teaching awards exist as well. Competitive summer teaching grants allow faculty to pursue new and innovative teaching techniques and curriculum revisions. Each year, the college awards 20 to 30 grants. Typically, one-half go to faculty who work with undergraduate students, and the rest are awarded to graduate faculty. The guidelines for these awards are straightforward: Concentrate on incorporating technology, active learning, and continuous quality into classroom efforts. In addition, the MBA programs sponsor a grant program that provides money for equipment and materials such as videotapes, computer disks, or special materials and supplies. Travel grants are divided between those attending professional meetings and those participating in training programs in quality and in cooperative and active learning.

Annually, the college singles out one undergraduate faculty member, one graduate-level instructor, and one teaching assistant for their teaching efforts. Each receives a plaque and a $1,000 savings bond from the Business Alumni Association. These excellence awards recognize outstanding competency in content area, clarity and creativity in articulation and expression of ideas, awareness of student needs, organization and conduct of classes, and willingness to interact and assist students. Students, student organizations, alumni, department chairs, and college support groups nominate faculty for the awards (Smith 1993a). At the doctoral level, teaching awards are being developed that will carry with them substantial honoraria and possibly an additional graduate assistant for the year.

To encourage teaching excellence, the college dean has initiated a procedure for identifying faculty with particular performance problems. The process targets faculty who, over time, receive below-average student evaluations and helps them develop effective teaching tools through education and mentoring. A plan for improvement, developed by the faculty member and his or her associate dean and department chair, might include in-house training in cooperative, active, and skill-based learning and in teaching methods, or involve having the faculty member sit in on the classes of fellow instructors and observe what they are doing in cooperative learning. A potential shortcoming in the college's overall thrust for teaching effectiveness, which may reveal itself in the future, stems from the lack of systematic teaching development across all faculty. Outside of the faculty who teach the core or those who have been identified as having inadequate teaching skills, most professors do not discuss classroom methods on a regular basis, especially across disciplines.

Improving student persistence. To address severe attrition rates among minority students in the undergraduate pre-professional core courses, the college initiated the Business Enrichment Program. Participants are members of ethnic minorities who enroll as freshmen or sophomores in a three-course block, which includes an introduction to business, microeconomics principles, and a humanities class called Contemporary Issues in Humanities. Within the business course, students form study partnerships for the other courses, practice college survival skills, gain a better understanding of the college's academic requirements and policies, explore opportunities provided by campus organizations, and learn how to seek out and apply for internships and scholarships.

The emphasis throughout this early intervention is on teamwork. As part of the enrichment program, the undergraduate advisement center offers DESKLAB, which requires that students spend a minimum of ten hours per semester working on either skill improvement, if remediation is needed, or on computer-related activities, if college preparatory work is not required. In addition, MBA students serve as mentors throughout the year. Students who participated in the Business Enrichment Program in its first year achieved a higher grade point average than did all other COB freshmen and, on average, completed more credit hours (COB 1994c; Lomeli 1993; Wolverton 1995).

The emphasis throughout this early intervention is on teamwork.

At the MBA level, building community among students and faculty plays a crucial role in the college's strategies for encouraging student persistence. Before entering the program, students are encouraged to attend an MBA boot camp, which consists of a series of minicourses for those who need an overview of basic core concepts. A weeklong orientation for the day program includes outdoor experiential training designed to strengthen group camaraderie and psychological testing to aid in team formation (MBA Program Office 1994).

During the year, faculty, students, and MBA staff interact at regularly scheduled coffee hours and other social events held in the MBA student lounge. For instance, this past year, pizza forums, where ten to 12 students met with faculty every other week, provided vital feedback for the program. In addition, a newly formed alumni MBA Council regularly meets with students. A Student Relations Committee, whose members include four local MBA alumni, two staff members, and five current MBA students, serves as a bridge between the program and the council. The committee hosts business tours, executive shadow days, and job workshops that focus on interviewing, professional attire and etiquette, resume writing, and networking. The committee also set up the summer internship program and a student-alumni mentorship program. In 1994, the council created an emergency loan fund to provide no-interest loans to MBA students who need short-term financial assistance *(MBA Council* 1993). Unlike their undergraduate and master's level counterparts, doctoral programs have yet to address the issue of student persistence.

Financial resources. The business college found that moving toward TQM required money. In its particular case, external funding eased the financial pain of transition for the college. For example, the Dean's Council of 100 generated the initial funds for Business Partners and continues to raise funds for summer teaching grants. A $250,000 matching grant (one of ten) from the Accounting Education Change Commission enabled the development of the accounting undergraduate teaching program. Over a five-year period, the accounting school had between $500,000 and $1 million at its disposal. Similarly, Hewlett-Packard awarded a $100,000 computer grant that allowed the college to convert from mainframe and DOS-based processing to UNIX-based workstation networks. With these changes in place, the college is developing state-of-the-art undergraduate and graduate decision-information systems curricula (Smith 1993b; Wolverton 1995).

Leadership and structure. The college's dean regularly communicates and reinforces his commitment to quality and a customer focus through meetings, speeches, and written communiques. Internally, he meets each semester with the faculty and staff to advise them of the college's accomplishments, the goals that remain unaddressed, the opportunities he sees for improvement, and new goals for the college. He conducts monthly meetings with faculty, semimonthly meetings with department chairs, and regular meetings with staff, students, and several groups that include members from outside the college. In addition to the Dean's Council of 100, the Business Partners, and the MBA Council, the dean meets with the Dean's Board of Excellence and the Business College Council. The Dean's Board of Excellence, a group of relatively new Phoenix-area business leaders, works closely with students in the undergraduate Honors Program. The Business College Council gives undergraduate students a voice in college developments. Externally, the dean meets on an ongoing basis with advisory committees, contributes to college publications, and emphasizes the college's commitment to total quality in presentations and speeches (COB 1994b; Wolverton 1995).

Operationally, the dean, associate deans, department heads, and center directors function in a manner that resembles a quality council. The group's main concerns center on educational quality, program improvement and design, program accessibility and advisement effectiveness, process stream-lining, resource allocation, continuous internal quality measurement (for example, customer audits, senior exit interviews, and the tracking of persistence rates and the time from entry to graduation), and external benchmarking against peer institutions (Wolverton 1995).

Closing comments

At the undergraduate level, administrators in the school of accountancy estimate that one-third of the faculty actively participated in the change process, another 15 to 20 percent have been somewhat active, and one-half have done nothing at all. Other departments seem to be following a similar scenario. In the MBA programs, although only 20 percent of the faculty are involved in the core courses, most electives closely follow the core format.

Some MBA faculty, however, have experienced difficulty moving across discipline-specific bounds. For instance, two instructors integrated their courses—one in strategic management, the other dealing with legal, political, and ethical issues—both part of the third trimester core. They then attempted to weave the integrated course into the entire first-year curriculum. The instructors met with other core professors and designed their integrated approach around the issues addressed in the other core offerings.

Between them, the two professors spent 72 hours in the classrooms of their colleagues during the first two trimesters. Their efforts were met with almost total indifference on the part of some faculty; others treated them as substitute teachers. Few instructors remained in the classroom and expressed an interest in working together on the project. Students refused to complete assignments because participation did not affect their grades until the third trimester. Whether faculty misunderstood the idea as it was conceived, believed that the curriculum was already too compressed and could not accommodate more material, or preferred not to collaborate for some other reason remains unclear (Jennings and Keller 1994).

As for the doctoral faculty, their associate dean sees an openness and a willingness to discuss issues that previously had been absent. She senses excitement and believes barriers are breaking down. The college's dean, however, considers moving doctoral faculty along the path toward CQI to be one of the greatest challenges the college faces. Even so, one administrator suggested that, overall, the percentage of the college's 175 faculty who "will never come on board" may be as low as 10 percent.

College of Engineering at Arizona State University: The Zealots and the Old Guard

The average age of the students in the College of Engineering is 27. Many students are married; most work 20 to 40 hours per week. Total college enrollment runs slightly more than 6,500, with 4,300 undergraduates. The persistence rate through graduation is less than 20 percent. Minority student participation sits at around 20 percent. Nineteen percent of the undergraduate students are women. Engineering is organized around six departments: chemical, bio, and materials; civil; computer science; industrial and management systems; mechanical and aerospace; and electrical. The majority of the college's 220 faculty teach undergraduates.

The impetus for curricular change in the baccalaureate program came from a group of concerned faculty who convinced the college to invest in a 1992 study to ascertain the future needs of engineering education. One faculty member suggested, "The idea was not to let industry or anyone else tell us what courses and topics to teach. It was to let them define the characteristics of the students as they graduate from our programs and then assess and measure whether or not our process produces the desired product."

Based on the responses from four customer groups—students, industry, society, and faculty—the study concluded that current graduates enter the workplace with insufficient capabilities in problem recognition and solution synthesis. They lack adequate communication and teaming skills, have little knowledge of business and management practices, and possess rather pessimistic attitudes about life in general (Bellamy 1993). Equipped with this information, the college entered into the process of curricular revision, and a small group of faculty began exploring the heretofore uncharted waters of TQM.

Three engineering faculty and one from psychology took part in Boeing's team member and team leader CQI training program in Seattle. Two of them then visited Mt. Edgecumbe High School in Sitka, Alaska, where students and faculty approach education from a quality management perspective.

Some of the faculty began familiarizing themselves with the concept of active learning by attending workshops offered through ASU's faculty development office. One chemical engineering professor later spent a semester-long sabbatical working at Mt. Edgecumbe. As he put it, "After our experiences at Boeing, ASU, and Sitka, we saw how cooperative learning, building student teams, and using quality management principles meshed to assess and improve the [learning] process." The instructor added, "The Sitka experience taught me that students meet whatever expectations we place on them; our expectations are low" (J. Matthews 1993a). The three-pronged approach to engineering education delivery that resulted was incorporated into an integrated, sophomore-level curriculum, which Texas A&M University had recently developed (see Bellamy and Raupp [1993] for curricular details).

ASU's process: The student

Traditionally, by focusing almost entirely on improving teaching and revising curriculum, the faculty controlled the learning experience but did not necessarily engage the students. Under ASU's new paradigm, faculty began to see themselves as facilitators who ease the learning process. One instructor observed, "We are adapting TQM to the classroom, not in the form of total quality teaching but as total quality learning. Our goal focuses on replacing the 'sage on the stage' with the 'guide on the side'" (J. Matthews 1993a).

To this end, ASU's delivery system depends heavily on a pedagogy that combines active learning, team building, and self-assessment (McNeill and Bellamy 1994b). The evaluation system represents the greatest departure from traditional educational approaches and, as such, proves to be the most controversial component of the paradigm.

The system employs Bloom's taxonomy of cognitive learning and Krathwohl's effective educational objectives. The centerpiece of the process is its competency matrix. The matrix plays a continuum of seven cognitive levels of learning and three degrees of effective internalization against a set of competency categories (educational goals) and a series of competencies (learning outcomes) for each category. Table 3 defines the learning levels. Figure 1 illustrates the basic matrix configuration.

The person responsible for setting course objectives and designing the learning experience and assessment instruments

Sample Competency Matrix

| Before Class | • | After Class | (shaded) |

Learning Outcomes	Competency Categories	comp #	Affective Degree			Cognitive Level					
			Receiving	Responding	Valuing	Knowledge	Comprehension	Application	Analysis	Synthesis	Evaluation
1. differentiation	exponential functions	1.1									
	hyperbolic functions	1.2									
	implicit	1.3									
	polynomials	1.4	•								
	trigonometric functions	1.5									
2. team meetings	code of cooperation	2.1									
	constructive feedback	2.2									
	devils advocate	2.3									
	gatekeeper	2.4									
	norms	2.5									
	team facilitator	2.6									
	team leader	2.7									
	team member	2.8									
	time keeper	2.9	•			•					

constructs the matrix and establishes grading guidelines. For instance, the instructor indicates an assumed initial state of learning for each concept and decides what level of learning a student must reach to meet the expectations normally specified for a B or C grade. A student must document performance above and beyond these specifications to receive an A.

A Guide to Self-Evaluation and Documentation of Educational States with Deviations (McNeill and Bellamy 1995a; see also McNeill 1994a, 1994b) explains the reasoning behind competency-based evaluation, the importance of student participation in the process, and the particular activities in which students will engage as a result of their involvement in the process. General information about the levels of learning and the degrees of internalization, including lists of process verbs that are associated with each learning level or degree (see table 4), an array of five questions designed to guide students through the assessment process, and specific engineering learning scenarios, helps students become actively engaged in determining their learning progress. One such example reads, "If you are in statics and can work single concept problems located at the end of specified sections, you are at the know-how level of learning for the current statics topic, because what you are doing matches the type of activity a person at that level of learning would be doing. On the other hand, if you are writing reports on the design of a bridge, you are probably at the synthesis level of learning for statics, because creation of evocative reports is an activity done by a person at that level of learning" (McNeill 1994a, 1994b; McNeill and Bellamy 1995a).

The student-driven documentation process generates a substantial paper trail that includes portfolios, reflection and work logs, run charts, and the competency matrix. All homework, quizzes, tests, reports, and projects are organized in a sequential portfolio or design notebook. In reflection logs, students explain why selected technical work shows that the student is functioning at a particular cognitive or affective level of learning for a specific competency. Work logs record when the work was done, how much time was spent, and where the work is located. Each entry also provides a brief description of the work. Run charts display the running average for a specified activity, such as class attendance, in graph form.

The competence matrix serves two purposes. It shows the student's performance level, and it indicates the location of

TABLE 3

LEARNING LEVELS AND DEGREES OF INTERNALIZATION

Levels of Learning

Before Knowledge: The student lacks familiarity with the topic.

Knowledge: The student possesses basic information about the topic but cannot explain the concept.

Comprehension (Know-How): The student understands and can explain the concept.

Application: The student can apply the concept or information to different situations in different contexts.

Analysis and *Synthesis:* The student can play with the concept, break it apart, and create new variations.

Evaluation (Appreciation): The student has a deep appreciation for the concept.

Degrees of Internalization

Receiving: The student can briefly summarize points from the presentation.

Responding: The student feels comfortable with his or her team and invests the expected effort for the class.

Valuing: The student believes that the material learned is useful and helps him or her solve problems (McNeill and Bellamy 1994a).

TABLE 4

SAMPLE PROCESS VERBS

Levels of Learning	Process Verbs
knowledge	define, label, memorize
comprehension (know-how)	describe, recognize, identify
application	apply, illustrate, operate
analysis	break apart, examine, explain
synthesis	arrange, construct, formulate, create
evaluation	appraise, judge, evaluate, compare

Degrees of Internalization	Process Verbs
receiving	concentrate, listen, recognize
responding	calculate, write, discuss, make, organize
valuing	care, convince, use

technical work to support the claim. The black dots in the matrix (see figure 1) indicate the cognitive and affective levels the student is assumed to possess already. The gray areas represent the levels he or she is expected to reach by the end of the semester. The white areas point to levels that the student might achieve (McNeill and Bellamy 1995a).

To demonstrate how the verification process for cognitive competencies might occur, consider the following example taken from an early version of the student-evaluation guide. The student's first assignment of the course is to work problem one in statics, which involves determining an unknown force acting on a simple beam. The student's work becomes the first two pages of his or her portfolio.

The next step is to determine which competency categories the assignment addresses. In this case, the student's ability to work the first statics problem indicates that he or she may possess know-how in two competency categories: free-body diagrams and equilibrium. When the student believes he or she has mastered this level of learning, he or she makes an entry in the reflection log. Each reflection log entry must identify which competency and level of learning (or degree of internalization) is being addressed, must give the location of supporting work, and must include a paragraph of reflection that explains why the student believes he or she has achieved the stated learning level. In this instance, it might read: Log Entry No. 1—Competency Category(ies): free-body diagram, equilibrium; Level of Learning: know-how; Location: portfolio, pages 1–15; Reflection: "Problems 1 through 10 each requested a free-body diagram and told me to use the idea of equilibrium of forces to determine the unknown force. Since the problems pretty much told me what to do and I was able to do it, this is evidence of know-how but not application" (adapted from McNeill 1994a).

Documenting competencies in the affective domain takes the student on a different tack. Here, students keeps two types of records—one chronicling the amount of time spent on class assignments and class-related activities, the other dealing with classroom behavior, such as timeliness and preparedness. On Sunday evenings, students use the data collected during the week to update run charts that depict class attendance, promptness, class preparation (reading), class assignments, and the average hours per week (outside of class) spent on class work. Once the student arrives at a specified degree of internalization, he or she substantiates his or her assertion in the reflection log (McNeill 1994a; McNeill and Bellamy 1995a).

In addition, each student keeps a personal journal in which he or she is encouraged to jot down reactions to, and feelings about, the class, its students, and its teacher as well as ideas, theories, concepts, and problems as they relate to specific topics. These journals are updated three or four times per week and periodically discussed with the instructor (McNeill and Bellamy 1994a).

ASU's process: The faculty

To accommodate the new learning approach, faculty changed classroom management styles. Participating faculty invest time in faculty development seminars that deal with active learning techniques. The faculty team, which participated in Boeing's training program and two more—one at Rio Salado Community College and the other offered by David Langford (Sitka)— holds workshops for other faculty on the basic precepts of team building. Tools to aid in classroom operation have been developed. They include lesson and team-meeting agenda planners, a generic classroom code of conduct, and a sample strategy on how to transform educational goals into educational outcomes.

Lesson planners help faculty organize their work by cognitive and affective learning objectives. In addition, planners serve as a systematic guide for staying on task by stipulating time allotments, equipment needs, room arrangement, learning group size, and delivery method. Perhaps the planner's most useful feature is a section reserved for after-class comments. Team-meeting agenda planners assist students and faculty in maintaining focus in meetings. They bear some resemblance to lesson planners but add information about the specific roles that team members will assume (Bellamy 1994; Bellamy et al. 1995; Bellamy and McNeill 1994).

Classes, in which competencies in quality principles, teaming, and the use of quality tools are not educational goals, often use a code of conduct to guide classroom management. As a starting point, the instructor provides a list of 15 to 20 statements, such as "Every member is responsible for the team's progress and success; there is no rank in the room; and have fun." The code is modified and expanded throughout the semester by the students and instructor to fit the needs of the class.

The strategy for translating educational goals into educational outcomes that McNeill and Bellamy (1994a) suggest involves breaking down an educational goal into increasingly specific and concrete parts using a conventional tree diagram. At each level of detail (or branch), the instructor answers the question: How will this be accomplished? When he or she arrives at a set of outcomes that can be achieved by someone else, the tree is complete. For example, an engineering professor who teaches statics and wants his or her students to learn how to design roof trusses might develop a tree in the following manner. The most general academic category from which all branches spring is engineering science. More specifically, engineering science breaks down into five narrower fields—thermal fluids, mechanics, electrical sciences, materials science, and material balances. At a more particular level, mechanics can be subdivided into three subcategories—statics, dynamics, and deformable solids. If we expand the statics branch, we find topical areas like frames, trusses, other structures, and ropes and pulley. Finally, for an engineer to design trusses, he or she must understand certain methods for configuring sections, members, and joints (see figure 2). For sequencing the tree, learning precedence must be followed—knowledge before comprehension, comprehension before application, and so on. Consequently, in our example, knowledge of statics and dynamics serves as a prerequisite for comprehension in deformable solids.

The results: A global initiative
Both ASU and Texas A&M tested the Texas-content/Arizona-delivery approach to engineering education. Based on their initial success, the two universities entered into a coalition with Texas Women's University (Denton), the University of Alabama (Tuscaloosa), Rose-Human Institute of Technology (Terre Haute, Indiana), Texas A&M University at Kingsville, and the Maricopa County Community College District (Phoenix). The coalition is funded by a five-year, $15 million matching grant from the National Science Foundation. It aims to fundamentally change the content and delivery of undergraduate engineering education and to improve the retention of engineering students—female, minority, and disabled students in particular. ASU's participation in the coalition, accord-

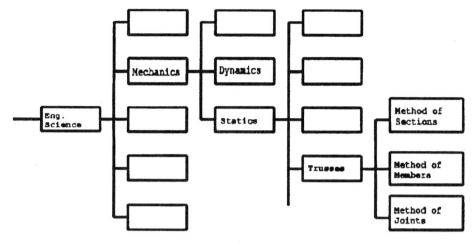

Tree Diagram

ing to one of ASU's co-principal investigators, will require
future collaborative work with the mathematics, physics, psychology, and humanities departments and the university's
Writing-across-the-Curriculum program (J. Matthews 1993b).

The results: Student performance

At the local level, one instructor's experience speaks to the
paradigm's potential. He related what happened once he
changed his approach. "If you look at first-day enrollment,
my lifetime student attrition rate is about 47 percent (in with-
drawals and failures), and it may be higher if you consider
the fact that many students never show up in my class because
they know better. If I teach back-to-back classes . . . one in
four students gets through. In my initial class under the new
system, I didn't lose any [students]. . . . The second semester,
I lost only one. . . . (Other faculty had similar experiences.)
. . . I realized then that while I had maintained high academic
standards throughout all my years of teaching, I had done little
to enable my students to meet those standards."

This instructor organizes his students into four-member
teams. He expects them to work as teams outside the classroom; in the evenings, he drops by their scheduled meeting
places to observe their teaming process—"Do members have
assigned roles? Are team members using the social norms that

they agreed upon? Is there an agenda? Is the meeting productive? Are they having fun?" At the request of students in this first class, the professor met every Saturday with two members of each team, who alternated their attendance every other week. In four hours, these students (in teams) discussed any material that either had not been covered in the previous week's class sessions, was unclear, or was not included in the competency matrix. The students then reported back to their colleagues. The instructor admitted, "To be honest, I didn't like spending all my Saturdays at school, but how could I say no when I had people who wanted to learn and were willing to commit their time?"

The students in this class did well; 80 percent earned A's. Other faculty became incensed. Not only had the program's "gatekeeper" defected, he had "gone over the edge and was giving away grades." In some circles, the instructor and his students became known as "the zealot and his Waco-ites." Although teacher and students had dedicated roughly twice the number of contact hours to course content as deemed necessary by traditional standards, the old guard refused to acknowledge the possible connection between effort and achievement.

The following year, four of the students from this class enrolled in an advanced science course. Because the class size was over 300 and the format was lecture, these students decided they could make more effective use of their time by having one person attend class, record the lecture, restructure and organize the notes, and present the material each week to the other three. Upon further reflection, a revised plan garnered even greater economies of scale. Each student recruited three other people in the class and formed a new team. The students taught their new initiates what they knew about teams and took them through a short version of the social norms used by teams. Together, they worked through the course. Their former instructor noted, "To me, my students are doing more than just receiving information: They're responding to it and valuing it. And some of them are making it a part of their value structure. I've never seen this kind of change in my students before."

The results: Faculty resistance
Although a number of professors place great stake in a multi-faceted paradigm that combines active learning, teaming, and

quality, resistance runs high. When one faculty member posts quality materials and notices about quality conferences outside his office door, another takes them down. When several instructors renovated their classrooms so they would be conducive to teamwork by bringing in circular tables, others referred to the rooms as the kindergarten classrooms.

Explanations for the resistance vary. On the surface, simple logistics appears to be the cause. "Everything we do takes time. . . . Faculty are used to spending a minimal amount of time on student- and classroom-related activities, some time on research, and the rest doing whatever they want to do. What we're doing threatens them." At a deeper level lies a philosophical desire to perpetuate the theory-versus-application dichotomy. Engineering faculty at ASU may be at odds with their counterparts in local industries like Intel and Motorola, where "if you can't work on a team, reach consensus, and be productive without getting your way, you don't work." The thought of student-faculty teaming to promote student ownership in the learning process seems foreign.

Deeper still, this pedagogical approach may challenge academic life as faculty now experience it. At issue are the concepts of student self-assessment and faculty sponsorship rather than ownership of the learning process. As one engineering faculty member observed, "There is incredible power here, very little responsibility, and no accountability. . . . We set up admission standards, which our students meet. We lose half of them, and we simply choose to believe that it's a problem with the supply. . . . If I worked in industry and you framed what's taking place here [at ASU] as an engineering problem—say, we have this process and the feed to the process is pretty constant, and over the years the product has begun to degrade (which is what has been happening here), what's wrong? And I tell you it's the feed, you would fire me."

The results: Taking another tack
Rather than promote a major paradigm shift, supporters have begun speaking to other faculty about the approach's sequential rather than concurrent aspects. So far, about 40 instructors have become comfortable with the techniques of active learning. As active learning activities grouped students who did not know how to work together, faculty began to view team training as a logical extension. By fall 1994, most had partic-

ipated in team training and were in the process of incorporating it into their classrooms.

Peer assessment, self-assessment and the levels of learning, active learning, teams and team training, quality, and TQM were standard components of the fall 1994 freshman core course syllabus. As of fall 1995, all freshmen must complete this course. The sophomore course is in place, and several junior-level courses dovetail with the freshman course but move the levels of learning to a higher plane. Some senior-level courses also use the format. In the 1994 fall semester, 10 percent of all courses offered by the college operated under the new framework. By fall 1995, the proportion was to increase to about 25 percent, but it remains unclear how much progress will be made after 1995.

As one faculty member remarked, "Some of us really did internalize this and there is no way back for us."

Closing comments

In 1994, the college's dean took a position at another university, and many believe that his departure hurts future prospects. In their eyes, the speed with which the college moves away from traditional content and delivery styles to methods framed by quality principles will depend heavily upon the new dean. Estimates of the number of faculty who will never alter their approach to teaching run as high as 40 percent, but those involved in change at ASU's College of Engineering believe that the quality paradigm works and that their numbers will increase. "We're pretty confident that we'll turn out a better citizen and we'll turn out a better engineer if industry really wants a team-oriented, quality-oriented, knowledgeable employee. If quality dominates American industry, we will be able to produce people that are much better able to contribute to and grow with it. If the quality paradigm dies, we may have to rethink this."

For some, their personal direction remains clear. As one faculty member remarked, "Some of us really did internalize this and there is no way back for us. I don't care how much flack I get. I can see that I have to do this."

Northwest Missouri State University: The Silent Pioneer

In any given year, 6,000 students enroll at Northwest Missouri State University, which is located in a rural community of 10,000. Most students attend full time, 90 percent are undergraduates, and 50 percent live on campus. The median age is 19; relatively few (11.6 percent) are married. The faculty, 246 strong, work with a predominantly Anglo student population, many of whom are first-generation college students. Eight departments—agriculture, human environmental sciences, art, mass communications, accounting and finance, marketing and management, curriculum and instruction, and psychology, sociology, and counseling—account for more than 60 percent of its baccalaureate graduates (NWMSU 1994a).

In 1984 under the direction of its president, NWMSU began to explore TQM. To align programs with the needs of the area it serves, the university consolidated seven colleges into four, which emphasize agriculture, business, and teacher education. By eliminating 31 programs, four full-time dean positions, and two vice president positions, Northwest reallocated $1.9 million (more than 6 percent of the education and general budget) to quality improvements in instruction (Hubbard 1994; NWMSU 1994c). These moves caught the attention of faculty.

Institutionwide quality initiatives

As the president observed, "With faculty, we started not with TQM but with a question. . . . What are the changes we need that would create a culture of quality in this campus? . . . We started by trying to figure out what were some core values and concepts for undergraduate quality . . ." (Marchese 1994). Consensus emerged around the following points:

- Quality education is talent development.
- High expectations are a starting point for quality.
- Learning is an active, not a passive, process.
- Assessment must focus on the prevention of failure and the improvement of instructional processes, not ranking and sorting.
- Instruction should be holistic, connecting subject matter to the world of work while challenging students to utilize all levels of cognition.
- Curricula should promote sustained interaction and teamwork between students and faculty.
- Time on task is an important consideration when improving education quality (NWMSU 1994a).

A steering committee built on these ideas, the input of faculty and students, and an extensive review of education-reform literature to formulate a strategic "culture of quality" plan.

Since the plan's adoption in 1987, most of its 40 goals and 42 action steps have been completed (Hubbard 1994). Through incentive awards (each worth $3,000), the university encourages the use of a seven-step planning process by departments to identify and validate key quality indicators; to develop and assess strategies to accomplish goals centered on meeting or surpassing the indicators; to establish baseline data, track trends, and benchmark superior processes at other institutions; and to stretch set goals (Weymuth 1994). All departments now have quality indicators. Most programs have customer-oriented advisory councils, and of the 97 undergraduate degree programs offered at Northwest, 69 have nationally normed major field exams available (NWMSU 1994a).

Northwest's planning process views instruction and its three key components—curriculum, teaching/advising, and the living/learning environment—as the university's core process. Today, a set of 17 institutionwide instructional goals embrace such notions as instilling the ability to listen actively for comprehension, evaluation, appreciation, and empathy; promoting an understanding of the workings of government and the political process; fostering the exploration of personal values, talents, interests, and lifelong aspirations; cultivating an international and multicultural understanding of the social, political, and economic conditions under which groups function; and encouraging the development of a capacity for self-directed learning. Together, they guide faculty in their attempts to improve the quality of education. With these goals in mind, faculty created and initiated a core curriculum that students must complete by the end of their sophomore year. The core includes a freshman seminar and courses in composition, oral communication, mathematics, computer literacy, life values, and physical fitness.

All colleges offer the seminar and individual colleges, depending on discipline, house the remaining core courses. For example, students take the computer literacy course in the business college and life values and physical fitness from the College of Education (NWMSU 1994c). A uniform course outline/syllabus format ensures that the goals are integrated into the objectives of core classes, and a 72 percent increase in writing assignments allows faculty to emphasize goals as they pertain to course content (Hubbard 1992, 1994).

In addition, the university lengthened each semester by two weeks and, in the fall of 1987, brought on line the nation's first comprehensive electronic campus. Terminals in every office and residence-hall room link faculty and students. To inculcate students into its "culture of quality," one week before their freshman year students participate in activities that introduce them to the university's expectations of their students. In this way, Northwest Missouri creates a collegewide atmosphere that encourages learning (Hubbard 1992).

The university also established student-assessment procedures, which are managed by the Talent Development Center. These procedures accomplish three goals. First, all entering students are assessed to set initial personal benchmarks, which govern course placement. Second, a set of national norms allows the institution to set high expectations for its students. In a recent interview, the university president summarized his sentiment about this type of benchmarking: "Comparisons of one's students or programs with those of other institutions is the best antidote for the inertia that plagues most campuses" (Marchese 1994). Third, at the end of the sophomore year, mandatory testing, combined with the analysis of a student writing sample, gives the university a means by which to measure the university's ability (through its students) to meet or exceed its established benchmarks. To date, more than half of all departments also have adopted or developed comprehensive senior exit exams, the results of which are used to evaluate program effectiveness but not to determine graduation (Brigham 1994; Hubbard 1992, 1994; NWMSU 1994a).

To support its faculty in their quality endeavors, NWMSU offers workshops to help faculty develop pedagogical strategies for extending writing, thinking, and listening skills across the curriculum. For instance, because faculty are encouraged to challenge their students to use analytical, synthesizing, and evaluative skills but few college instructors systematically learn how to construct questions that test different cognitive skill levels, the university brought in specialists for weekend workshops (Hubbard 1994).

In another instance, Northwest conducts yearly teaching workshops for new faculty unexperienced in teaching at the college level. On occasion, but not always, professional development opportunities involve the introduction of TQM tools. In addition, Northwest provides funding for faculty and staff to attend externally sponsored workshops on quality, and it awards applied research grants that give faculty the chance to experiment with new approaches to quality instruction (Brigham 1994).

Specific classroom examples

In 1984, NWMSU began offering a course in computer literacy. Today, 25 sections give students access to this core requirement. Traditionally, faculty discussed problems, sounded out ideas, and introduced new software to each other, but few shared course materials. With the aid of a culture-of-quality grant, a small group formed a team to develop improved materials.

In the fall of 1992, all course instructors were invited to participate in the effort. All accepted. The amount of work assigned to a faculty member corresponds to the number of sections taught. (For example, a person teaching three sections has three times as many duties as a person teaching a single section.) Team members were assigned to tasks depending on their strengths. Some wrote exams, quizzes, lab exams, or the final; others worked on the syllabus and on coordinating the course. To ensure quality, all versions of quizzes and exams are proofread by two instructors other than the original author. The result: high-quality materials and minimal duplication of effort as far as material preparation is concerned (Detmer 1994).

Faculty in the College of Arts and Humanities have two projects under way. Known as Alpha and Beta, these projects track groups of undergraduate students to assess the effects of alternative combinations of teaching and learning experiences. Each group is compared to a control group to determine similarities and differences in curriculum development and the way in which various general education courses address institutional goals, issues of multiculturalism, and good teaching practices (NWMSU 1994b; Weymuth 1994).

The lifetime wellness team consists of nine faculty who use a common syllabus that includes the course's description, objectives, performance indicators, grading scale, and topical outline. They use the same exams, study guides, and textbook. Each team member is considered an authority in one of the nine course content areas and, as such, provides the learning objectives, performance indicators, exam questions, media sources, related literature, resource persons, and textbook review associated with his or her area of specialty. Where students are concerned, the faculty's overall goal focuses on enabling "students to realize their fullest human and health potentials to improve the quality and quantity of life" (Johnson 1994).

Closing comments
By the president's estimation, "The most important step we took was beginning with the faculty" (Hubbard 1994). His administrative assistant adds, "By plan, we tried to be sure that every person in the university is aware of our quality initiatives. This does not mean that all are involved equally. Some are only minimally involved, others are very active . . . (probably 30 percent or more serve on committees that deal with specific quality projects) . . ." (Weymuth 1994).

Today, a review committee consisting of students, faculty, staff, and community works to update the strategic "culture of quality" plan using the Malcolm Baldrige Award criteria, and Northwest plans to realign the budget with the key quality indicators submitted by the deans of each college. As a result, faculty will have more say over money spent on faculty development and equipment (Brigham 1994).

Samford University: The Student-First Quality Quest
Samford University, a private, Southern Baptist–affiliated comprehensive university in Birmingham, Alabama, enrolls approximately 4,400 students, a quarter of whom are graduate students. Samford's reasons for embracing CQI were primarily internal. Both the president and provost believed that the university needed to pursue a strategy of "organized betterness" (Brigham 1994). As the assistant to the provost for quality assessment, who serves as the quality coordinator, noted, "Samford's president . . . was a leader ready for TQM to happen. His focus on students as customers is tied to his understanding of marketing in higher education . . ." (Harris 1993). The president named Samford's quality effort "Student-First Quality Quest" (SFQQ) and brought the assistant to the provost for quality on board in 1989 to coordinate SFQQ (Harris 1992).

One of the coordinator's first moves was to develop a semester-long course that focuses on the basic ideas of TQM rather than specific tools. To support these efforts, the president and provost wrote papers that dealt with such aspects as customer orientation and servant leadership, which helped faculty see the link between total quality concepts and their respective academic disciplines (Harris 1993). By the spring of 1992, some orientation to TQM had been provided for everyone on campus.

In addition, Samford's leadership team, the president's quality council, spent one day per month studying and discussing TQM. In the seventh month, an external consultant walked the team through an exercise in quality planning called mission-customers-processes-values-vision (MCPVV). After almost two years, a draft of Samford's MCPVV was distributed to all faculty and budget heads for comment. A year later, every unit used the university's MCPVV as a point of reference.

Simply put, Samford's mission challenges the university to "nurture persons—faculty, staff, and students"—through learning experiences. Its vision dares the university to "develop a [new] model rather than replicate another. . . ." Every unit uses MCPVV in planning and budgeting procedures. With the help of the assessment, planning, and budgeting (AP&B) panel, comprising faculty and staff, all departments and units developed assessment methods that seek input on the alignment of mission, values, and vision and on process effectiveness (Harris 1993).

Putting TQM to work in the classroom
Nursing. Traditionally, pass rates on the licensing exam for registered nurses ran between 90 and 100 percent, but in February 1989, the rate dropped to an unexpected 45 percent when a revised exam was put in place. Turmoil erupted among the faculty. One group blamed another. Some boosted personal popularity with students by publicly eroding students' confidence in other faculty and openly expressing their determination to rid the school of its new dean. By spring 1992, however, several faculty had resigned, and with the help of the quality assessment office, the school began a search for causes. Many thought that the problem lay with the transfer students (Brauer 1993).

However, an analysis of grades and test scores uncovered no significant difference between transfer and other students. Instead, investigation revealed that the program was admitting unprepared students; that courses lacked proper sequencing, causing students to miss crucial competencies altogether; and that much of the instruction and classroom testing emphasized note taking and memorization, while the new test focused on problem solving and analytical reasoning. In fact, in a course that she taught, the dean found that students were unable or unprepared to discuss assigned readings from the text, and they seemed unable and unwilling to make inferences or use deductive methods because they were totally dependent on the instructor to lecture (Brauer 1993).

Based on their findings, faculty changed curriculum, scrutinized existing recruitment and admission criteria as well as the admissions process itself, and resumed responsibility for ongoing academic advisement. Subsequently, enrollment doubled and attrition declined. Today, the pass rate again hovers close to 100 percent (Brauer 1993).

Department of Biological Sciences and the School of Nursing. The Department of Biological Sciences offers a biology course as a service to nonbiology majors, such as nursing. Traditionally, very little interaction ever took place between the biology department and the School of Nursing. After receiving quality-improvement training, the department decided to concentrate on customer service, process, and statistical analysis. It began by surveying one of its customers— the nursing school. It discovered that nursing had been monitoring the effectiveness of the biology course through the National League of Nurses (NLN) board exam for anatomy and physiology and that poor student pass rates on the exam were a major concern (Baggett 1992).

An academic quality team, which included the professor who taught the course, the department chair of biological science, the dean of the School of Nursing, and the chairs of the nursing school's curriculum and admissions committees, diagrammed the nursing program's academic process using a flowchart to identify where biology fit into the overall schema. With standardized flowchart symbols (boxes denoting tasks, diamonds decision-making junctures, ovals starting and ending points, and so on) connected by arrows that indicate the flow of the process, the team mapped the academic path a nursing student at Samford typically takes. Before entering upper-division nursing courses, all students pass through the biology course. This suggested that failure of students to do well on the anatomy portion of the nursing exam in some way related to the degree of success that they had in the biology course (Baggett 1992; Hunsinger 1992).

The team brainstormed to uncover the nature of this relationship and to generate possible root reasons for test failure.

Potential causes included not enough hands-on experience, which might stem from a lack of access to cadavers and organ models in the biology lab; inadequate pre-NLN exam review sessions, which could be a procedural problem; pressures on faculty to pass along students, which might indicate that longstanding policies should be revisited; and poor study habits, ineffectual instructors, or simple scientific ineptness, all of which could be considered personal shortcomings (Baggett 1992; Hunsinger 1992).

Once these ideas surfaced, the team developed a cause-and-effect (or fishbone) diagram. At the head of the spine (of the fish) lies the problem—low NLN scores. The supporting ribs—equipment, policies, procedures, and people—branch at angles from the spine. From each rib, hair-like bones organize the root causes. For instance, a lack of cadavers sprouts from the equipment rib, pressures to pass along students from the policy rib, inadequate formal pretest review from the procedural rib, and poor study habits from the people rib. Based on their ability to array the information in a meaningful way, the team formulated three goals—reduce the number of failures, strengthen the mastery level of the C students, and increase the performance on the exam (Baggett 1992; Hunsinger 1992).

Pareto analysis of available data produced a bar graph that plotted the number of students scoring poorly on the NLN exam against four independent variables—course-test time lag, grade earned in the biology course, student ACT/SAT scores, and whether the biology course was taken elsewhere. The analysis showed that the variable that correlated most closely with poor NLN scoring was the long time period that elapsed between the completion of the anatomy and physiology (biology) course and the actual administration of the NLN exam (Baggett 1992; Hunsinger 1992).

Team members charted a plan of action using a Plan-Do-Check-Act (PDCA) cycle. They redesigned the nursing school academic process, set timelines for implementation, executed the changes, assessed the results, revised the process, and adopted the changes on a permanent basis. Specifically, they increased admissions standards, required that prerequisites for the anatomy and physiology course be established, and administered the NLN examination immediately upon course completion. As changes went into effect, scoring patterns consistently improved, and a feeling of cooperation, teamwork, and pride among quality team members emerged (Baggett 1992; Hunsinger 1992).

Education and psychology. Other colleges have used quality concepts to design programs and courses or incorporated them directly into their classrooms. For example, student leaders and faculty developed an elective course titled Quality Leadership, which is offered in the School of Education (Brigham 1994). In psychology, faculty invited eight students to form a quality team. All members were psychology majors who had expressed an interest in being involved. As their first task, the group, through brainstorming, determined that the ideal class setting was one in which students experienced a minimal level of fear (Teal 1992).

The psychology class studied fear, and the team interviewed their classmates to find out what causes fear in the classroom. They used Pareto charts and cause-and-effect diagrams to diagnose specific situations and constructed a flowchart of the fear process. Students agreed that deconstructing fear in a systematic manner took away some of its ambiguity and mystique. By the end of the exercise, some already had acted to reduce their own fear levels (Teal 1992).

The Schools of Nursing, Education, Pharmacy, Music, and Arts and Sciences. The dissertation work of a doctoral student provides a final example. The student designed and piloted a manual for student quality teams in conventional classes. Using the LEARN manual, three to five student volunteers collect information from class participants about what is and is not working. They **L**ocate an opportunity for improvement, **E**stablish a team, **A**ssess the current process, **R**esearch causes, and **N**ominate a solution (Cornesky 1993). Because the feedback occurs early in the semester, the instructor can take corrective action while the course is in progress. Faculty in accounting, biology, and mathematics piloted the process during the 1992 summer session. Currently, faculty in the Schools of Nursing, Education, Pharmacy, Music, and Arts and Sciences use LEARN, and the manual is being tested at several other institutions. Samford's provost hopes to eventually replace end-of-course student evaluations with LEARN teams (Brigham 1994).*

---

*More information about the LEARN manual can be obtained from Dr. Kathy Baugher, Dean of Admissions, Belmont University, 1900 Belmont Boulevard, Nashville, TN 37212-3656.

Closing comments

Samford has been least successful in promoting and using cross-functional teams. Faculty quickly soured on the idea when they discovered that much time and energy could be wasted on problems that did not warrant such expenditures. One successful venture, however, has been the freshman experience. The team, comprising the vice president for student affairs, the dean of arts and sciences, the dean of academic services, the head of the biology department, the campus minister, the director of student activities, and the director of the Freshman Forum, worked two years on the project (Harris 1992, 1993).

To begin, the team researched the basic literature on late adolescent, early adulthood, and student development. Using an affinity diagram to generate a list of possible student and university needs and expectations, the team outlined those concerns that could be best addressed during a freshman experience. To develop the affinity diagram, team members submitted handwritten suggestions, continually rotating through the group until all possibilities had been exhausted. The handwritten suggestions then were collated by category— student needs, student expectations, and university expectations.

On the basis of this work, the group developed a survey for freshmen and their parents. The survey's analysis revealed concerns that led to two major changes. First, participation in the Freshman Forum became voluntary, and course content was aligned to respond to the needs of Samford students. Second, freshman orientation was given a more academic emphasis. Subsequently, the activities of the freshman year were reconfigured to academically challenge students and, at the same time, take student and parent needs and expectations into account (Harris 1992, 1993).

. . . the activities of the freshman year were reconfigured to academically challenge students and . . . take student and parent needs and expectations into account.

Although some faculty remain only minimally engaged in Samford's Student-First Quality Quest, many are beginning to view the university as a "web of interconnected processes" (Harris 1993). To this end, Samford is employing the Malcolm Baldrige National Quality Award criteria to facilitate the assessment process for its SACS 1994–1996 reaccreditation (Brigham 1994).

Maricopa County Community College District: Making the Leap to Quantum Quality

MCCCD is the second largest multicollege system in the country. As such, its ten community colleges and one skill center serve approximately 180,000 credit-seeking students yearly. Another 30,000 individuals enroll in noncredit courses and, in partnership with Motorola University, 21,000 more participate in noncredit training programs. The district employs more than 870 full-time and approximately 2,500 adjunct faculty. Students who transfer from the Maricopa district make up 51 percent of Arizona State University's upper-division enrollment. Forty-six percent of ASU's baccalaureate degrees are awarded to former district students (MCC 1994).

In 1992, following a one-year pilot program at Rio Salado Community College, Maricopa embarked on its journey into continuous quality. Although fiscal constraints, which forced substantial budget cuts, coincided with the district's instigation of "Quantum Quality," it decided to sidestep higher education's more traditional administrative and support-service entry points. Instead, Maricopa, under the guidance of its chancellor, cut to the quick by inaugurating Quantum Quality systemwide and systemically deep into its core—the teaching/ learning environment.

Campus presidents, many of whom had little input into the decision to adopt TQM into their academic operations, questioned its applicability. Faculty immediately raised cries that Quantum Quality threatened academic freedom, but a more pointed reason behind faculty reticence may well lie in Quantum Quality's perceived threat to a lockstepped pay system in which rewards are tied to education attainment and longevity of service. To calm Maricopa's potentially troubled waters, the district's steering committee, the Quantum Quality Executive Council, issued a statement that the quality initiative would not impact the faculty work agreement (Brigham 1994). As a consequence, faculty resistance, for the most part, remains passive.

Unlike many college TQM training efforts, which segregate administrators from faculty and staff, Maricopa includes members of all three categories in each training group. Even though participation in training opportunities is voluntary, most college officials agree that the response has been excellent. To promote clear communication, MCCCD initiated a weekly electronic-mail Quantum Quality update. During the last two years, the college has invested considerable time in an attempt to redefine its vision and mission in terms of Quantum Quality (QQEC 1994).

Rio Salado Community College

In contrast to the other colleges in the district, Rio Salado has no permanent campus, recruits only adult learners, hires few full-time faculty, actively seeks out innovative delivery alternatives, and purposefully encourages course development based on current student needs (Wolverton 1991). Its employees—ten full-time faculty, 130 support staff, and 450 to 650 part-time instructors—serve the needs of 28,000 credit students and 10,000 noncredit students by offering classes at more than 250 sites throughout the county (RSCC 1994a). Ninety-three percent of Rio's students are working adults who are building their career skills (RSCC 1991a). The average student is female, between the ages of 26 and 36, and married.

More than half of Rio's students are new each semester (Wolverton 1991). To address this issue, faculty and administrators recently conducted an intensive telephone campaign. Shortly before classes began, they called students from the previous semester who had not registered for the current term and encouraged them to take another class. One out of seven students contacted reenrolled; people at Rio attribute their success to the college's constant attention to customer service (Thor 1993).

The ten full-time faculty serve as discipline specialists and provide the Rio "glue." Each year, they coordinate course work, scrutinize and approve course content (ensuring consistency across the system), and supervise and support (with the help of part-time mentors) part-time faculty. Rio selects its adjunct faculty on the basis of expertise and looks for professionals who are excited about teaching. The vast majority are employed full time elsewhere and are hired by Rio on a per-semester basis. By using such short-term contracts and periodic classroom observation and evaluation, Rio believes it can ensure quality in the classroom (Wolverton 1991).

From its inception in 1978, Rio was never meant to be a place but a system. To create Rio, the five existing district colleges relinquished responsibility for 240 courses that were being offered off campus using part-time staff. By employing this cost-effective approach to expansion, the district avoided $60 million in construction costs but raised the ire of both the colleges that previously housed these programs and faculty who had not been involved in making a decision that directly affected them. To this day, hard feelings exist, especially among those colleges that were most vocal in 1978—Glendale, Phoenix, and Scottsdale (Wolverton 1991).

The college embraced TQM in 1991 because its new president wanted to introduce more horizontal leadership and increase institutional efficiency and responsiveness. A steering team guided the implementation of TQM within Rio Salado, and a quality coordinator oversees the day-to-day management of the initiative (Brigham 1994). By 1992, the college's geographically defined organizational structure proved cumbersome under the new system and was reconfigured totally along functional and program lines.

Rio's vision statement identifies the college and its members as leaders in total quality. Its mission statement challenges the college to pursue continuous improvement in all that it does (RSCC 1994a). To this end, all full-time faculty and staff and about one dozen part-time faculty participated in 40 hours of project team training. Some now are moving through a follow-up, 40-hour sequence. Most part-time faculty members have been exposed to four hours of CQI awareness training. When surveyed in 1994, 56 percent of Rio's part-time instructors said they were using quality materials and tools in their classrooms.

The college offers degrees and certificates of completion in quality process leadership and quality customer service. Courses dealing with TQM and quality principles are listed in the catalog under the general heading of Total Quality Management or as significant components of a number of business courses. The college customizes training to fit specific company needs and conducts the training at the firm's facility when this arrangement is more convenient to the company. The college's Quality Academy strives to help organizations learn to do more with less and is dedicated to "delivering education and training in TQM and CQI for business, government, education and medical organizations, and communities" (RSCC 1994b). In 1993, Rio Salado became one of eight winners of the Arizona Governor's Award for Quality, the Pioneer Award.

Putting Quantum Quality to the test: Bringing it into the classroom

Nine principles of quality learning guide much of the district's Quantum Quality classroom efforts. Four, in particular, exemplify Maricopa's approach.

- Quality Learning is defined as meeting or exceeding the internal needs of the instructor, the discipline, and the college (grading criteria, competencies syllabus, curriculum, credits, etc.), and the expectations of the students (learning, environmental, teaching methods, grading, testing, and 'value added').
- Quality Learning is everyone's responsibility; therefore, the instructor and the students form a team that makes decisions that focus on the students' achievement of the competencies.
- Students want to be involved and will make decisions that increase the quality of their own learning.
- Quality Learning is a continuous process of improving the critical processes for each team—that is, each group of students and their instructor.

Student outcomes reflecting course competencies and program goals are measured by grades, course completion rates, employer satisfaction, and transfer rates. Student goals are measured by retention, surveys, and employer satisfaction (RSCC 1994c).

The action plan model. At Rio Salado Community College, faculty members follow an action plan model based on TQM—its principles, tools, and continuous improvement cycle—that takes the team through a structured problem-solving process. The continuous improvement cycle steps include planning activities, data collection, implementation of the change, measuring the effect, and standardization of the change. It is a teacher-guided, data-based, student-focused process that can help the instructor and the students define priorities to be addressed through a cooperative effort. TQM tools aid in each step. For example, students might develop a cause-and-effect diagram, like the one in figure 3, to help them understand why they have difficulty following directions.

Working together to improve. An instructor at Rio Salado more fully illustrates this process. The instructor sees TQM as ". . . a vehicle for student success." In her classroom, students function as teams, help set course goals and strategies, and continuously modify and improve them (Assar 1993). When she discovered students were taking up to six hours to complete a five-point project that should have been a two-

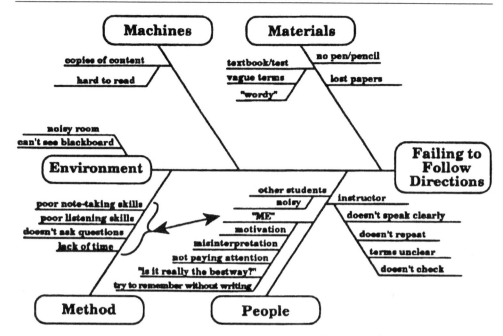

Machines
- copies of content
- hard to read

Materials
- textbook/test
- vague terms
- "wordy"
- no pen/pencil
- lost papers

Environment
- noisy room
- can't see blackboard

Method
- poor note-taking skills
- poor listening skills
- doesn't ask questions
- lack of time

People
- other students
- noisy
- "ME"
- motivation
- misinterpretation
- not paying attention
- "Is it really the best way?"
- try to remember without writing

Failing to Follow Directions
- instructor
- doesn't speak clearly
- doesn't repeat
- terms unclear
- doesn't check

hour activity, the instructor and her class used Rio's structured approach to decrease the total time spent on class projects without jeopardizing product quality. "The students and I worked together to collect data on time spent and grades received. The students asked specific questions of each other regarding the work processes that were used during these assignments. Then, as a team, we drafted a change in the wording of the project directions, which resulted in less student effort in completing the tasks. Data were collected again on time spent and grade received. The result was that two-thirds of the students had decreased their work time by at least 30 percent while grades remained high or increased" (Helminski 1992).

Class management. Rio's quality coordinator teaches psychology. "In my classroom, I place more emphasis on the philosophy and principles of quality than on the tools. If the content lends itself to them, then the tools are a nice benefit. In fact, we often use cause-and-effect diagrams." The first night of class, she and her students discuss the principles and what they mean to her as an instructor and to her students as learners. They also develop ground rules for the classroom, with the list posted at every class meeting. As a living document, it can be modified at any time. Each session ends with class participants completing a plus-delta exercise—what worked well in the class that night and what did not. (A delta indicates that room for improvement exists and a change needs to occur. A plus suggests that an activity should be added to the learning experience.) The instructor also asks students to do plus-deltas on themselves as learners—were they prepared, did they participate? She checks these personal plus-deltas several times during the semester. In each case, students and instructor try to eliminate their individual deltas (see figure 4).

TQM: One of many tools. The department chair for health enhancement and an instructor in the applied business department at Phoenix College believes that TQM is just one more tool that helps create learning communities. As a teacher, the chair combines TQM, cooperative learning, active learning, and collaboration into an all-encompassing umbrella. At the beginning of each semester, she and her students talk about the TQM principles and what they mean. They then develop the class based on the quality principles. "I tell students that this is their classroom. They're here to learn, and I'm here to facilitate that learning."

Feedback on Teaching/Learning during the class session
1) for the Teacher
2) for Yourself

+	△
1)	1)
2)	2)

Her class ground rules set the framework by which the instructor and students operate in the classroom. Typically, the rules include "a safe environment is one in which we respect one another; there is confidentiality; everybody has an opinion and it's all right to share that opinion. . . . The reality is that if students create their own parameters, they live by them." After the list is finalized, all students receive a copy. "We explore our expectations. I have a certain amount of content to teach, but the methodology by which that content is delivered differs depending on where the students are coming from. Always, my primary expectations are that we will have fun and that we will have a good semester."

This instructor consistently uses several TQM tools. One she calls "keepers." These are the "a-ha's!" of life, the "moments when the light bulb comes on." They may happen in class, at work, or at home. At the beginning of each class, she asks, "Are there any keepers?" Students then share the situation in which a course concept made sense to them. The teacher builds on their experiences. She often breaks her class into randomly assigned teams. In groups, they conduct brainstorming sessions, use affinity diagrams, or experiment with nominal group techniques to work on specific questions, issues, or projects in class. Through periodic plus-delta surveying, the instructor regularly gathers data about how the learning environment can be improved. She notes, "I don't think that using quality concepts (or TQM) in the classroom is something that is new. We're just calling what we do by a different name. . . ."

Closing comments

The district estimates that full institutionalization of Quantum Quality will take five to ten years. Thorough and expedient training about the nature of change in general and about TQM in particular is deemed key to successful integration. To date, Maricopa's most tangible results come from Rio Salado. The college's penchant for experimentation, innovation, and creativity; a cadre of full-time faculty that is substantially smaller than those found at other colleges; and a president who champions TQM efforts may well combine to give Rio its leg up.

Overall, faculty responses to the district's commitment to TQM have been mixed—idealistic enthusiasm, especially among those at Rio Salado, counterbalanced by cynicism and categorical dismissal. In fact, faculty at one of the district's largest colleges, Glendale Community, voted unanimously not to participate. Support for the district's move to quality improvement among campus presidents varies. Most, however, seem skeptically optimistic about the future prospects of Quantum Quality at Maricopa (Assar 1993).

Miami-Dade Community College: Broadening The Definition of CQI

Miami-Dade functions as a single college with five campuses scattered throughout Dade County, Florida. The student population of more than 60,000 is 52 percent Hispanic, 20 percent black non-Hispanic, and 24 percent white non-Hispanic. The college has the largest international enrollment in the country. Of its total student population, about 75 percent begin their studies at Miami-Dade with deficiencies in at least one scholastic area. Presently, 70 percent of the faculty are full-time employees. Within the next ten years, the college expects one-third to one-half of its veteran faculty to retire *(Miami-Dade* 1993).

The college and its people do not think of Miami-Dade as a TQM organization. But, K.P. Cross (an authority on classroom assessment) has termed the Teaching/Learning Project at Miami-Dade "an excellent example of the idea of total quality management" (Cross 1993). She draws a parallel between the purpose that lies behind TQM and the reason why faculty engage in classroom assessment—a major component of the project. Both deal with continuous process improvement through ongoing assessment. In Miami-Dade's case, the process is learning and the objective is not to punitively evaluate teaching but to improve learning through instruction.

Prior to the Teaching/Learning Project, Miami-Dade engaged in what it terms the first wave of reforms. This was a series of reforms designed to assess and place students in courses in which they could build the skills they needed for success in more traditional college-level work. A core curriculum and a computerized advisement and articulation system also were added. In 1985, the college was designated the top community college in America, a distinction it still enjoys. In 1986, the institution embarked on the Teaching/Learning Project (Wolverton 1994).

The project ties a comprehensive professional development program to a faculty-designed advancement system in an attempt to impact the classroom effectiveness of its teachers and the quality of learning of its students. The development program includes graduate courses, orientation and mentoring for new faculty, and fully staffed resource centers on each campus. The college pays all tuition and supply costs for those who enroll in the graduate courses, and new faculty receive a stipend for participating in orientation as do mentors for fulfilling their duties.

The advancement system awards continuing contract, tenure, promotion, and endowed teaching/chair positions based on teaching portfolios. At three-year intervals, faculty prepare portfolios, which originally consisted of annual performance reviews, student survey summaries, and self-assessments for three years, optional peer reviews, a narrative, and documentation of 29 faculty attributes. The narrative and documentation sections proved troublesome because some attributes were not easy to document, and both subsequently were modified. Today, portfolio preparers answer questions about motivation, interpersonal skills, knowledge base, and knowledge base application and document their answers with specific classroom-related materials. All project components, which once focused entirely on full-time faculty, have now in some way spilled over to affect adjunct faculty, administrators, and support staff.

Similarities in the Teaching/Learning Project and CQI
The project and CQI can be compared along several dimensions, such as the drive for continuous improvement, the desire to increase employees' involvement, or the pursuit of process consistency. However, four—customer orientation, standards of excellence, faculty development, and rewards—in particular, stand out from the rest.

Customer orientation. While students at Miami-Dade seldom are referred to as customers, the approach to teaching and learning taken by most faulty is decidedly customer oriented. The nature of Miami-Dade's fundamental charge—to provide access to higher education—and the extreme diversity of its student population make it essential that faculty have a keen sense of the community they serve. As one faculty member put it, "We're not only talking about where [students] come from and what their background is. . . . Our responsibility deals with where the students will be ten years from now."

To further this sense of responsiveness, the project introduced a measure of faculty accountability into the scheme of things at Miami-Dade. Students complete evaluative surveys in each class during the college's major semesters after the first half of the term but before the final date for withdrawal. Many faculty agree that the college's focus on quality has intensified and that the student evaluations have been the moving force behind the Teaching/Learning Project. As one instructor commented, "[Because of them] all of us are now forced to look at every aspect of what we do."

Another reflected, "I think it comes down to a question of changing behavior. [For instance,] on the first round [of student surveys] the results showed that I wasn't questioning students in class. I changed my behavior and checked to see if I rated higher in that area the next time around. I did." In a similar vein, an instructor discovered that she speaks too rapidly and now keeps reminding herself to slow down. Faculty on other campuses made similar discoveries. One said, "I found that there were some things that I thought I got across to the students, but I didn't. . . . The next semester I did a better job."

As the project progressed, employees in every work area of the college began to understand that how they performed their duties impacted Miami-Dade's learning environment. A senior administrator remarked, "To begin with, the prime focus was on faculty, what happened in the classroom. It's only in the latter stages that we've realized that the issues are much broader, that what happens in the classroom encompasses staff responsibilities, administrative responsibilities, how those things interact, and how closely interrelated the various elements of the college are to the teaching/learning mission of the college. So we've expanded the original conception." An incident in maintenance adds color to the administrator's comments. In response to complaints about dirty classrooms, faulty equipment, and burned-out light bulbs, Miami-Dade decided to treat faculty like "hotel guests." It set standards for the classroom and now attempts to anticipate rather than simply react to faculty needs (McCabe and Jenrette 1990).

Standards of excellence. Today, seven questions guide contract continuation, promotion, and tenure decisions at Miami-Dade. How faculty address these questions and document their answers determines their status in the organization. As one faculty member commented, "We now have indicators, standards that establish teaching as a priority . . . standards that cross all teaching disciplines." The questions:

- What challenging goals have I set for myself, and what progress have I made toward attaining them?
- How do I motivate students or others whom I serve?
- How do I interact positively with colleagues and students?
- How do I create a climate conducive to learning?
- How do I update my own knowledge, professional skills, and resources to make my instruction or service meaningful (professional growth activities)?
- How do I meet or support the individual learning needs of students?
- What information do I have that shows my students' achievement or the effectiveness of my service? (TLP 1993).

A close look at these queries reveals that they focus on the dynamics of the teaching/learning environment. The first two address issues of motivation; the third and fourth speak to interpersonal skills; the fifth one deals with acquiring, maintaining, and expanding a knowledge base; and the last two seek evidence of the application of that knowledge base.

Documentation still includes self-assessments, performance reviews, and student feedback. To them, classroom faculty add course syllabi, examples of tests and other assessment devices, descriptions of teaching strategies and samples of student achievement, or a description of how the teacher knows that his or her students have achieved. Nonclassroom faculty (for example, librarians) provide samples of informational materials, discussions of applicable projects and activities, and substantiation of any of the classroom requirements that pertain to their specific situations (TLP 1993).

Faculty development. Three pieces of the project's faculty development component bear considerable resemblance to education and training efforts that take place in highly effective CQI organizations. Miami-Dade and University of Miami faculty collaboratively developed two courses, which are mandatory for new faculty and optional for all others. In addition, the college instituted a mentoring program for new faculty and established learning centers on each campus.

Courses. The courses, one on classroom assessment and the other on teaching and learning strategies (especially those that are culturally specific), are offered twice a year at sites on the college's three largest campuses. Their effect has been substantial. For instance, following his completion of the classroom-assessment course, one faculty member began to invite fellow instructors into his classroom to collect feedback from his students, which he uses to improve what occurs in the classroom. "This is probably the first semester where I have used tools to actually empower my students to feel more involved in their own education. . . . I think that's great."

His revelation about his experience seems similar to those of many of his colleagues. One offered this example: "Last summer I started paying closer attention to the way I write my tests and prepare students for them. After each test, I now ask students two questions: Was the preparation for the test adequate? And was the test fair and the format agreeable? I tell them—don't just say, 'I hated it,' and leave it at that. Tell me what can be done to improve test preparation, the test format, or the test questions. . . . They're [the students] very happy with [this arrangement] and feel that they're learning much more. It shows in their progress."

A survey of the first classroom research course participants, three months after completion of the course, found that 84 percent continued to conduct some form of classroom research. Fifty-five percent had changed their teaching style as a result of feedback and research activities. One year later, a second survey showed that 61 percent continued to recommend the techniques learned to their colleagues, and most also indicated that the strategies presented in the course were practical and helpful in efforts to improve the teaching/learning process (Herrera 1989). A more recent survey showed that faculty and administrators who had successfully taken the classroom feedback course had shifted their emphasis away from exclusive attention to student achievement and learning skills and toward an assessment of their own teaching styles (Cuevas 1991).

A newly hired faculty member related the significance of the teaching strategies course. "You can take it for granted that one of the questions for new hires will be 'Can you function in multicultural environments?' and one of the things

"This is probably the first semester where I have used tools to actually empower my students to feel more involved in their own education. . . . I think that's great."

that the course made us aware of is the fact that students [from different cultures] learn in different ways." In addition, the course exposes participants to different teaching styles, the mechanics behind using such tools as audio and visual equipment, and student participation and projects. "We bring back new ideas from the course. . . . The rest [faculty] are starting to see that a lot more is going on now than did [a few] years ago."

Many find that the greatest advantage to participating in either class comes from the opportunity it gives them to interact with other faculty. For these faculty, the courses help them identify problems that students have in different departments and alerts them to how other faculty handle these problems.

Mentoring. The original intent of the mentoring component of the project was to "integrate new people into a tough, bureaucratic system." The unintended beneficiaries, however, seem to be the mentors. One mentor described his new charge: "He's so alive; he's a great model for what good teaching is. . . . I'm getting so much out of mentoring him." Another noted, "I sit in on their classes and they sit in on mine. I get observed every Monday, Wednesday, and Friday. I don't know if I am doing anything differently . . . but maybe because I have more people observe me, I do my act a little better. I say [to myself], 'What can I do today that they haven't already seen?' " A Learning Center director says, "It's like they get a shot of adrenaline."

Centers. Center directors design workshops and seminars based on faculty needs and interests. Faculty often seek the center directors' input on teaching strategies and course development. Minigrants awarded through the centers to fund faculty-generated projects also help capture the potential for improving student learning in the classroom. Faculty design computer software and interactive videos. As one instructor put it, "There are budgets for that now." A colleague described his current efforts: "I've submitted a proposal . . . for a minigrant for research in conjunction with a project going on in the U.S. Department of Education on new ways to evaluate student behavior. I want to try my ideas out in a pilot study. . . ."

Without reservation, faculty on all campuses agree that the centers provide opportunities to exchange ideas and develop friendships with people they otherwise might not see. One department chair noticed an even more direct result of the project and its centers: "Faculty are thinking a little more about . . . whether their students are learning and how much. . . ."

Rewards. To complement the college's faculty development program, faculty designed a reward system that compensates faculty who emphasize teaching and learning. To demonstrate competency, faculty prepare teaching portfolios, which are reviewed by faculty-dominated campus committees. All department chairs undergo extensive training in how to conduct performance reviews, and faculty evaluate the performance of the chairs in the performance review process.

Typical faculty reactions to the portfolio process go something like this: "I am reviewing everything; I have to look at these [originally 29 attributes, now questions] from a different perspective, a different angle, and it keeps me on my toes." Academic deans see all portfolios, both those submitted for continuing contract and those for promotion. All deans agree that they detect a difference in the quality and the kinds of things that the new faculty (who have taken the two graduate-level courses) submit—a level of sophistication in terms of how they approach teaching that is absent in many of the portfolios submitted by tenured faculty.

To recognize teaching excellence, the college awards endowed teaching chairs (also determined by a faculty-controlled committee, this time a collegewide one). Faculty compete for the endowed chair positions, and eligibility is restricted to full professors who have been at Miami-Dade for at least six years. A faculty member explains, "Most colleges that offer endowed teaching chairs award them to people from outside the institution. They come in, visit for a year, get a lot of money, and then leave. What we've done is start a program that rewards our own people for being good in the classroom." Approximately one-third of the 100 three-year positions are awarded annually. Each chair carries with it a $5,000 yearly stipend plus $2,500 expenses per year, both to be used at the faculty member's discretion (TLP 1992).

Behind the scenes: Leadership and wherewithal
The president at Miami-Dade began the project with a concept paper that outlined his ideas about how to enhance the teaching/learning environment. He presented it at a retreat

attended by more than 100 faculty and administrators. His only stipulation was that endowed chairs would exist; everything else was up for discussion and debate. A steering committee and a series of subcommittees worked on the project for five years before the final piece, the reward system, was fully operational. Widespread acceptance and ownership of the project's pivotal piece, the new policy guidelines, were deemed so crucial that an outline of advancement system changes was brought before the faculty in a two-day referendum (Cross 1993).

Fiscal resources were in some cases realigned to support the new processes and in others generated from outside sources. In its most active years when committee work was high, the project's budget stood at $220,000 to $230,000 per year. As subcommittee activity diminished, the budget decreased proportionately. Overall, campus-specific staff development budgets, which are channeled through the Learning Centers, increased by just under 20 percent. Capital spending also underwent restructuring. Early in the project, faculty raised the issue of office space. Few had areas in which they could consult privately with students, and many believed that this inhibited their ability to deal effectively with their students. Capital budgets for each campus were redirected to allow for the construction of faculty offices. The cost to date—about $1 million. In addition, the college built a privately supported $7.5 million endowment to fund the teaching chairs.

Closing comments

A few faculty who plan to retire within two to three years do not actively participate in faculty development opportunities, nor do they engage in the portfolio process. Fellow instructors assume that they either "don't want to be bothered, don't want to be questioned," or simply resist on the grounds that the advancement process "infringes on their academic freedom." But peer pressure to become involved is extreme, and for the most part, faculty seem to have settled into the college's new routines. Veteran instructors are energized and new faculty are excited. Sam McCool, new faculty member at Miami-Dade and coauthor of several books on TQM, said it best: "I wanted to experience the opportunity of teaching at an institution that is truly dedicated to quality teaching."

SUMMING UP

To this point, this monograph outlines the basic premises of CQI and catalogs frequent reasons why quality efforts fail. It then describes continuous quality initiatives at seven organizations of higher learning that have, to a certain degree, managed to circumvent some of the pitfalls that commonly haunt quality endeavors. This section considers the commonalities that cut across all of these activities, the characteristics that some, but not all, of the approaches share, and those features that are unique to one particular institution.

Common to All
Customer focus
Each of the colleges directly confronts the issue of customer image. In all the cases, there is either a new focus on or a heightened awareness of "the customer." Most define their customers as students, alumni, and area employers. Because NWMSU faced the prospect of progressively restrictive budget constraints, it needed to build local support and did so by structurally reorganizing to reflect the primary employment groups of the region—agriculture, education, and small business. Consequently, of the case study organizations, Northwest Missouri seems to be the college most concerned with the expectations of local industry.

At the Maricopa County Community College District, although the immediate threat of severe financial shortfalls coincided with its adoption of Quantum Quality, the district claims that money was not the main motivating factor behind its moves—that, instead, the concerns of its clients played a significant role in Maricopa's quality initiative. The colleges at ASU responded to industry-specific studies, the Graduate School of Business at Chicago to a report of alumni dissatisfaction in *Business Week.* Samford University sensed a "need to do better," which probably was stimulated by alumni and employers. Miami-Dade has, over time, exhibited a sensitivity to its external constituency that typifies most community colleges. Its Teaching/Learning Project does not, however, seem to have resulted from undo external pressure.

At each of the case study institutions, administrators referred to students as customers. This action, at least initially, met with faculty resistance at many of the colleges. The dean of Arizona State's College of Business noted a common reaction: "At first, I never mentioned total quality management or used the words 'students' and 'customers' in the same sentence. Now,

I can speak of students as customers without the faculty visibly flinching."

Commitment at the top: The role of leadership

No change occurs without leadership from someplace (Stewart 1994). At colleges where efforts to improve the way faculty functioned in the classroom met with the least resistance, top administrative leaders initiated the process of change. The president at Northwest Missouri State, the president and provost at Samford University, the president at Miami-Dade, and the dean of ASU's business college to this day remain actively involved in their institutions' attempts to enhance classroom effectiveness.

Maricopa County Community College District illustrates the importance of leadership's buying in on the project. At Rio Salado, the college pursued TQM because its president wanted the college to do so. At the district level, considerable time and effort have been devoted to bringing Quantum Quality districtwide, because the chancellor sees the merit in such action; but at individual colleges (other than Rio) the internalization of Quantum Quality has met with mixed success, because campus presidents were told to adopt Quantum Quality whether or not they were committed to the notion.

At the two institutions that experience the lowest levels of faculty participation and the greatest degree of faculty indifference—the Graduate School of Business at the University of Chicago and ASU's engineering college—the deans, while supportive, have not actively participated in their colleges' efforts to improve quality. Some of what the engineering college is experiencing may reflect the philosophical schism that exists among the university's top administrators. The president favors the expansion of ASU's Total Quality Service beyond the confines of college support services. The provost for academic affairs does not see its relevance to the classroom.

Classroom and curriculum

Not surprisingly, since it was one of the criteria for selecting the case study institutions, all institutions focus on classroom effectiveness. Effectiveness seems to be measured in terms of student persistence, at least at Samford and the business college at ASU. Others, such as the College of Engineering and Miami-Dade, focus more on learning and learning outcomes. Most are involved in curriculum revisions, although this is not the case at Miami-Dade and appears to pertain only to Rio Salado in the Maricopa District. In Rio's case, TQM programs were added to current course offerings.

Customized faculty development

Each college engages in training or education that suits its specific situation. Some efforts—for example the Maricopa County Community Colleges, particularly Rio Salado, and Samford University—concentrate heavily on introducing the principles and tools of quality management to faculty. The Graduate School of Business at Chicago through its Teaching Laboratory, Northwest Missouri State University, and ASU's business college add in-house exposure to active learning techniques. Faculty in the College of Engineering train their colleagues in teaming, but they look to the university's faculty development office for instruction in active learning techniques. Miami-Dade developed graduate-level courses that focus primarily on active and cooperative learning methods but do not include exposure to TQM tools.

Faculty development at most of the case study institutions seems to cover the nuances of classroom assessment—especially at Samford, where LEARN student teams assess faculty classroom effectiveness, and at Miami-Dade, where classroom research serves as a principal cornerstone of faculty development. Generally, faculty seem to downplay the traditional emphasis of TQM (or CQI) on the statistical control of variance in favor of more personalized adaptations, such as the personal quality checklist. Where statistical tools like Pareto or run charts are employed, applications seldom move beyond rudimentary frequency tabulations or simple graphing.

Cost in time and money

Finally, all institutions seem to realize that internalizing continuous quality takes time. Northwest Missouri and Miami-Dade both have been engaged in their efforts for at least ten years, Chicago and Samford for five years or more. No one at any of the colleges spoke about quick answers or short-term fixes. All case study organizations made substantial financial commitments—either realigning current fiscal resources or finding new sources of funding. The pointed remarks of one engineering professor at ASU reflect a common sentiment: "Changing to a quality paradigm may cost, but when you realize that we scrap or rework as much as 60 percent of our potential product, you begin to understand just how great the financial and intellectual expense of the current paradigm really is."

Characteristics of Some Quality Efforts
Catchy nomenclature
The participating schools and colleges at Chicago and Arizona State refer to their approaches as simply TQM. Rio Salado Community College also uses the term TQM. The Maricopa District, however, coined the phrase Quantum Quality to capture the essence of its program. Northwest Missouri State University has its Culture of Quality, and Samford pursues the Student-First Quality Quest. Miami-Dade's label is straightforward—the Teaching/Learning Project. Based on this sampling, program or initiative name seems to carry less weight than might otherwise be expected.

Quality responsibility
The existence of a quality office sometimes indicates that quality efforts are a parallel process to the rest of the organization (Numerof and Abrams 1994). This may be true at Chicago, where a quality office handles students' suggestions and coordinates quality teams formed in the teaching lab. By channeling its initiatives through a special office, Chicago may be insulating the majority of its faculty from any disruptiveness caused by attempts to integrate CQI into the classroom. The degree of faculty resistance experienced by the College of Engineering at ASU strongly suggests that, at least in the beginning stages, the TQM movement took shape as a parallel initiative.

The Maricopa District has no district-level quality coordinator and officially proclaims that "quality is everybody's responsibility." Individual campus response to Quantum Quality suggests, however, that some of them may not accept the district's corporate view of responsibility. Samford and Rio Salado employ part-time coordinators. Miami-Dade has an office of Teaching/Learning Advancement. Neither the College of Business at ASU nor Northwest Missouri State hires a coordinator. In each case, the organization emphasizes the communal nature of responsibility.

Standing student advisory groups
Only the business colleges seem to formally recognize standing student advisory groups. In the case of Chicago, students

are involved directly in curricular reforms like LEAD and the suggestion box, but much of what they do pertains to non-credit course work. At ASU, students serve a more program-matic advisory role. Other case study colleges use students in more ancillary capacities, such as classroom assessment and course evaluation. In all cases, although faculty adjusted their courses when possible to meet the needs and expec-tations of their students, the instructors retained final say over content determination.

Faculty participation

Faculty participation varied from case to case. Northwest, Sam-ford, the business college at ASU, and Rio Salado experience fairly substantial levels of involvement that appear to be grow-ing. Faculty response in the Maricopa District as a whole remains mixed. Participation is high at Miami-Dade, but it is confined to relatively few faculty members at Chicago, where progress is slow, and in ASU's College of Engineering, where resistance is strong.

If we consider all seven organizations (eight with Rio Salado counted separately), each has willingly spent time and money on its quality efforts and invested in faculty develop-ment. They all focus on students as customers and direct their attention to the classroom. The degree of top-level adminis-trative involvement seems the most notable difference in the approaches taken. Where the role of leadership goes beyond providing support to hands-on engagement in the process, faculty participation seems greater. At Chicago and ASU's engi-neering school, where administrators are only passively in-volved, personal revelations about the value of the approach taken and about how faculty changes can affect student learn-ing seem to steel dedicated faculty champions in the face of peer disapproval.

Baldrige and benchmarking

Institutions that experience widespread faculty involvement develop comprehensive approaches that include some pro-vision for measuring progress. For instance, the College of Business at ASU, Rio Salado Community College, Northwest Missouri State University, and Samford University evaluate their programs using Baldrige criteria. Northwest Missouri and ASU's business college have applied for state awards that are comparable to the Baldrige Award. Rio Salado won Arizona's award in 1993.

Although Miami-Dade's efforts are not tied to the Baldrige criteria, the college does monitor its Teaching/Learning Project. The project received national recognition for its excellence in 1993, when it garnered the Theodore M. Hesburgh Award for faculty development. In the cases of the College of Engineering and the Graduate School of Business at Chicago, we see little mention of using the Baldrige criteria as an evaluative tool, perhaps because strides for CQI have not been ingrained collegewide.

Assessing effectiveness under the Baldrige criteria involves benchmarking, and the College of Business at ASU, Northwest Missouri, and Samford all benchmark. Maricopa talks about benchmarking. While Miami-Dade does not employ the CQI benchmarking techniques that some of its counterparts use, the college continuously pays attention to the actions of other institutions of higher education. It does not, however, systematically try to emulate other institutions; instead, Miami-Dade hopes to serve as a benchmark for its peers. Neither Chicago nor the engineering college seems to actively engage in benchmarking activities.

Uniquely Different
In certain instances, unique components have been introduced that either hold the potential for, or have resulted in, increased faculty resistance. For instance, the curricular approach at the College of Engineering, which requires extensive teaming, competency-based grading, and student portfolios that reflect the levels of cognitive and affective learning achieved, met with extreme defensiveness on the part of many faculty. The preliminary results, which promise improvement in student learning, seem to galvanize involved faculty in their resolve to continue in their continuous quality reforms.

Miami-Dade took perhaps the most radical approach when it redefined its reward and advancement systems to reinforce desired changes in faculty behavior. Although some Miami-Dade faculty held misgivings, most engaged in the change process because newly designed opportunities for faculty development gave them the tools they needed to meet the new expectations, and the reward system recognized their efforts. In contrast, Maricopa's promise to leave the salary and reward structure intact may have acted as a disincentive to faculty.

Samford's move toward LEARN-trained, student term evaluation teams and away from standardized individual course evaluations sets the institution apart from the rest. It remains to be seen, however, whether team course evaluation is a practice that will become widely accepted or highly opposed.

UNANSWERED QUESTIONS

The cases presented point to classroom experiences, both curricular and instructional, in which the use of CQI (or a similar approach) seems to improve student learning. Common themes, such as customer focus and leadership commitment, emerge as forces that influence the degree of success that these colleges and universities encounter as they integrate quality principles into daily classroom operations and attempt to positively impact the learning environment. Undergirding each instance lie certain assumptions: educational quality needs to and can be improved, customers deserve a greater say about what takes place in the classroom, benchmarks and standards of quality can be set, CQI is now the way of American corporate life and education should follow suit. Often these ideas remain unarticulated and consequently go unchallenged. This final section gives voice to some of the misgivings lingering in the shadows of CQI.

One of the mainstays of CQI in business today is setting quality standards and then working to reduce process deviations to meet those standards.

Standardization

One of the mainstays of CQI in business today is setting quality standards and then working to reduce process deviations to meet those standards. To date, much of the effort in higher education to define these guidelines has been restricted to schools of business and engineering. In fact, the connection between industry and schools of business and engineering makes the transition to standards a natural extension of industry/education collaboration. Likewise, for some time engineering schools have taught the statistical tools necessary for gauging variation (Bateman and Roberts 1993). In addition, business schools have an added incentive. As a part of its accreditation process, the American Assembly of Collegiate Business Schools now requires that schools demonstrate how they use quality principles to improve curricula, faculty, and administration (Freed, Klugman, and Fife 1994). No matter what the reason, setting standards in either college appears relatively straightforward simply because outcomes often are readily measurable. After all, accountants need to be able to balance ledgers, and engineers must know how to apply the principles of dynamics to design issues.

But in other areas of study, who defines quality? Who sets standards and determines acceptable margins of variation? In education, does the consensus needed to create such standards stifle creativity that derives from reflective energy and insights and dialogues generated across differences? In a world of growing diversity, is CQI merely a way to reduce dissimilarity by forcing homogeneity?

Benchmarks and Customer Focus

Establishing benchmarks and serving the customer are hallmarks of CQI. But do these CQI essentials limit our perspective on quality? When we base our benchmarks on historical data, or even current information, can we push the limits of forward thinking? If customer-focus means customer-led, do we beg the questions of whom we will serve in the future and whom are we not serving today? Further, if we conform to present "client" expectations, are we ceding control that could later jeopardize academic freedom?

Customers, whether they are students attending college or their future employers, are notoriously lacking in foresight. Meeting only the articulated needs of customers may condemn an institution to the role of perpetual follower (Hamel and Prahalad 1994). In a society filled with organizational also-rans, should institutions of higher learning instead take the lead?

Teams

Teams may be the least understood and the most overlooked phenomenon of the current quality movement. Teams do not just happen. To be effective, they take time and energy and involve shared responsibility and mutual accountability, yet often people are thrown together with little or no training or support (Dumaine 1994). In education, we talk about student teams, faculty teams, and student/faculty collaboration. But do faculty and students know how to be team members?

When faculty successfully initiate a team approach to learning, what then? One undergraduate engineering student observed, "Team assignments are fine, but the faculty go about it in all the wrong ways. In the real world, you rarely find four electrical engineers teamed together. Instead, you find an engineer teamed with people from finance, marketing, and management. That's the kind of work situation we need to practice. . . ." What implications does such an observation hold for educators who typically work within the security of insulated discipline specialties?

Interdisciplinary Consequences

Failure to see the interconnectedness between actions taken by one part of an organization in the name of quality and the ramifications of those actions for another segment of the organization can cause problems (Manz and Stewart 1994). For example, when ASU's business college, under the flag of TQM, added the international component to its undergraduate program, students could select courses from several colleges at the university to fulfill the new requirement. As a consequence, a popular political science course on current issues in international politics, which is housed in the College of Liberal Arts and Sciences, suddenly was oversubscribed by 400 eager business college students. Prior notice from the business college of a possible heightened interest in international courses in other colleges would have given the political science department time to prepare and would have gone a long way toward avoiding the untenable situation that resulted.

By the same token, if student teaming in engineering falls short of its intended purpose, perhaps the same holds true for similar exercises undertaken in the College of Business. Coordination across colleges would be key to any attempt at forming interdisciplinary student teams. The question is raised: Can CQI be taken on in isolation?

Rewards

Whether we like it or not, money motivates our behavior. We do what we must to make a living. For some faculty, at least in the short run, what gets rewarded tells them what is important. In the case of large universities, tenure based on a faculty member's ability to publish may signal that research is the top priority. In smaller comprehensive universities and community colleges, the emphasis may be on community service. It stands to reason, then, that changing what we reward should lead to changed behavior. For instance, tying rewards to change goes a long way toward guaranteeing faculty participation at Miami-Dade: They either buy in or move on.

By the same token, faculty development targeted at desired faculty behaviors can provide the impetus for change. Indeed, a major component of the Teaching/Learning Project revolves around providing the tools and techniques that support faculty efforts to change or improve behavior. Assuming that our efforts will result in changed behavior and desired outcomes may, however, be an act of naive anticipation (Numerof and Abrams 1994).

To be sure, at Miami-Dade, we find a group of professionals historically paid less than their local K–12 counterparts who have experienced inconsistent offerings in faculty development. Yet in 1985, the year before the inception of the Teaching/Learning Project, Miami-Dade was ranked the top community college in the country. What motivated its faculty? It seems that more than extrinsic rewards come into play at Miami-Dade. In fact, Miami-Dadeans have traditionally valued the opportunity to be creative, to take risks without fear of recrimination, and to invest time in their students. By combining the advancement system and faculty development into a system, which sends clear extrinsic signals that classroom effectiveness counts, Miami-Dade supports its faculty as they pursue those activities they intrinsically value (Kohn 1994).

Where desired changes require ongoing teamwork and interdisciplinary collaboration, an even more complex quandary surfaces, because we pay individuals but expect team participation. In the end, what motivates faculty to engage in some activities and not others? Can we expect long-term gains in education quality if we fail to change our reward systems? If we change extrinsic remuneration, can we afford to ignore the role faculty development can play or the power of intrinsic motivation? By the same token, can we rely solely on intrinsic motivators to ensure changes in faculty behavior?

Paradigm Durability

Today, the quality paradigm is alive and well in American business, but does the movement represent a fleeting managerial fixation, a passing fancy, or a sustained drive? Over time, American industry (emulated by educational institutions) has moved from scientific management to management by objectives to strategic management. In a scramble for quarterly profits acquired through short-term efficiency and sustained through hierarchical control, U.S. industrialists continue to forfeit the employee ownership and commitment necessary for the long-term change espoused by current movements in process improvement. Can they shed such bottom-line mentalities? (Manz and Stewart 1994). Is CQI here to stay, or will educational institutions in their attempts to mirror industry climb aboard the CQI bandwagon just as business leaps into some new paradigm that holds the promise of economic well-being?

The Notion of Quality

To some, the introduction of CQI and its quality principles
as new ideas implies that whatever was done before was not
"quality." The truth of the matter may be far from it. Indeed,
many faculty believe that quality is what led education to the
prominent place it now holds in society—that, in fact, quality
is already reflected in the way educators function—and they
see no reason to change. To address this dilemma, proponents
of the quality paradigm advise us to tie revolutionary change
to enduring values (Hamel and Prahalad 1994; Kohn 1994;
Numerof and Abrams 1994; Stewart 1994). If the path to continued education quality entails monumental transformation,
we raise an even greater quandary than the one concerning
the pre-CQI existence of quality. Under the constraints of a
paradigm based on the concept of continuous improvement
and geared toward solving process problems, are we capable
of raising the kind of possibilities needed for thinking about
"revolutionary change"? Quality management asks how we
can do what we do better when the proper question may
well be whether we are doing the right thing. Simply put, is
CQI enough?

APPENDIX: Contacts by Institution

University of Chicago Graduate School of Business

Harry V. Roberts, Professor
The University of Chicago
Graduate School of Business
1101 E. 58th Street
Chicago, IL 60637

College of Business at Arizona State University

Larry Penley, Dean
Steven K. Happel, Associate Dean for Undergraduate
   Education
Barbara Keats, Associate Dean for Doctoral Programs
Lee McPheters, Associate Dean for MBA Programs

College of Business
Arizona State University
Tempe, AZ 85287

College of Engineering at Arizona State University

Lynn Bellamy, Associate Professor
Department of Chemical, Bio, and Materials Engineering
College of Engineering and Applied Sciences
Arizona State University
Tempe, AZ 85287

Barry McNeill, Assistant Professor
Department of Mechanical and Aerospace Engineering
College of Engineering and Applied Sciences

Northwest Missouri State University

Annelle Weymuth
Executive Assistant to the President
Northwest Missouri State University
800 University Drive
Maryville, MO 64468

Samford University

John Harris
Assistant to the Provost for Quality Assurance
Samford University
Birmingham, AL 35229

Maricopa County Community College District

Donna Schober
Executive Assistant to the Chancellor
Maricopa County Community College District
2411 W. 14th Street
Tempe, AZ 85281

Sharon Koberna
TQM Coordinator
Rio Salado Community College
640 N. 1st Avenue
Phoenix, AZ 85003

Miami-Dade Community College

Mardee Jenrette, Director
Teaching/Learning Advancement
Office of the President
300 N.E. 2nd Avenue
Miami, FL 33132-2297

REFERENCES

The Educational Resources Information Center (ERIC) Clearinghouse on Higher Education abstracts and indexes the current literature on higher education for inclusion in ERIC's data base and announcement in ERIC's monthly bibliographic journal, *Resources in Education* (RIE). Most of these publications are available through the ERIC Document Reproduction Service (EDRS). For publications cited in this bibliography that are available from EDRS, ordering number and price code are included. Readers who wish to order a publication should write to the ERIC Document Reproduction Service, 7420 Fullerton Rd., Suite 110, Springfield, VA 22153-2852. (Phone orders with VISA or MasterCard are taken at 800-443-ERIC or 703-440-1400.) When ordering, please specify the document (ED) number. Documents are available as noted in microfiche (MF) and paper copy (PC). If you have the price code ready when you call EDRS, an exact price can be quoted. The last page of the latest issue of *Resources in Education* also has the current cost, listed by code.

Ansoff, I. 1980. "Strategic Issue Management." *Strategic Management Journal* 1(2): 131–48.

Assar, K. May/June 1993. "Phoenix: Quantum Quality at Maricopa." *Change:* 32–35.

Astin, A. 1991. *Achieving Educational Excellence*. San Francisco: Jossey-Bass.

Baggett, J. 1992. "Demythologizing Quality Improvement for Faculty." In *Quality Quest in the Academic Process*, edited by J. Harris and J. Baggett. Methuen, Mass.: GOAL/QPC.

Bateman, G., and H. Roberts. 1993. "TQM for Professors and Students." Unpublished manuscript. Chicago: The University of Chicago. HE 028 432. 24 pp. MF–01; PC–01.

Bellamy, L. 1993. "Engineering Education at Arizona State University: Poised for Significant Change." *ASEE Conference Proceedings.*

———. 1994. Rose-Hulman Institute of Technology Team Training Workshop. Tempe, Ariz.: College of Engineering and Applied Sciences, Arizona State University.

Bellamy, L., D. Evans, D. Linder, B. McNeill, and G. Raupp. 1995. *Teams in Engineering Education*. Tempe, Ariz.: Arizona State University. HE 028 427. 250 pp. MF–01; PC–10.

Bellamy, L., and B. McNeill. 1994. *Curriculum Development, Design Specifications, and Assessment: Supplemental Materials*. Tempe, Ariz.: College of Engineering and Applied Sciences, Arizona State University. HE 028 446. 160 pp. MF–01; PC–07.

Bellamy, L., and G. Raupp. 1993. *NSF/Texas A&M New Engineering Science Core at Arizona State University*. Tempe, Ariz.: College of Engineering and Applied Sciences, Arizona State University. HE 028 446. 160 pp. MF–01; PC–07.

Bemowski, K. October 1991. "Restoring the Pillars of Higher Education." *Quality Progress.* 37-42.

Blakemore, A. March 1994. "Undergraduate Initiative: Improving Success and Diversity." Unpublished internal document. Tempe, Ariz.: Arizona State University.

Brauer, M. Summer 1993. "Bringing a Nursing Program Back to Life." In *Pursuit of Quality in Higher Education: Case Studies in Total Quality Management* (78), edited by D. Teeter and G. Lozier. San Francisco: Jossey-Bass.

Brigham, S. 1994. *25 Snap Shots of a Movement: Profiles of Campuses Implementing CQI. Part of AAHE's Continuous Quality Improvement Project.* Washington, D.C.: AAHE Publications. ED 378 887. 127 pp. MF–01; PC–06.

Chaffee, E. 1989. "Strategy and Effectiveness in Systems of Higher Education." In *Higher Education Handbook of Theory and Research,* edited by J.C. Smart. New York: Agathon Press.

Chaffee, E., and L. Sherr. 1992. *Quality: Transforming Postsecondary Education.* ASHE-ERIC Higher Education Report No. 3. Washington, D.C.: Association for the Study of Higher Education. ED 351 922. 145 pp. MF–01; PC–06.

Coate, L. July 1990. *Implementing Total Quality Management in a University Setting.* Oregon State University.

————. 1992. *Total Quality Management at Oregon State University.* Washington, D.C.: National Association of College and University Business Officers.

College of Business, Arizona State University. Spring 1992. "Update: Students Try TQM on for Size." *Business.*

————. May 1993a. "Strategic Plan for the College of Business." Unpublished internal document. Tempe, Ariz.: Arizona State University. ED 380 052. 10 pp. MF–01; PC–01.

————. Fall 1993b. *Arizona State University MBA Programs.* Tempe, Ariz.: Arizona State University.

————. 1994a. *A Strategic Plan for the Future.* Tempe, Ariz.: Arizona State University.

————. Spring 1994b. "Application for the Pioneer Award." Unpublished internal document. Tempe, Ariz.: Arizona State University.

————. Summer 1994c. "U.S. News & World Report Ranks ASU MBA Program 21st in the Nation." *Business.* 12.

————. Winter 1994d. "MBA News." *Business.*

Cope, R.G. 1987. *Opportunity from Strength: Strategic Planning Clarified with Case Examples.* ASHE-ERIC Higher Education Report No. 8. Washington, D.C.: Association for the Study of Higher Education. ED 296 694. 149 pp. MF–01; PC–06.

Cornesky, R. 1993. *The Quality Professor: Implementing TQM in the Classroom,* edited by J. Lind. Madison, Wis.: Magna Publications. ED 367 206. 202 pp. MF–01; PC not available EDRS.

————. 1994. *Quality Classroom Practices for Professors.* Port

Orange, Fla.: Cornesky & Associates.

———. March 1995. "Continuous Quality Improvement in Education." *The Chronicle of CQI* 1(1).

Cornesky, R., and S. McCool. 1992. *Total Quality Improvement Guide for Institutions of Higher Education.* Madison, Wis.: Magna Publications. HE 028 181. 166 pp. MF–01; PC not available EDRS.

Cornesky, R., et al. 1990. *Using Deming to Improve Colleges and Universities.* Madison, Wis.: Magna Publications. ED 354 838. 122 pp. MF–01; PC not available EDRS.

Cornesky, R., S. McCool, L. Byrnes, and R. Weber. 1991. *Implementing Total Quality Management in Higher Education.* Madison, Wis.: Magna Publications. ED 343 535. 154 pp. MF–01; PC not available EDRS.

Crosby, P. 1979. *Quality Is Free.* New York: McGraw-Hill.

———. 1984. *Quality without Tears.* New York: McGraw-Hill.

Cross, K.P. July 1992. "Assessment in the Classroom." *NCA Briefing.* Special Insert—Commission on Institutions of Higher Education 10(2).

———. February/March 1993. "Involving Faculty in TQM." *AACC Journal:* 16.

Cross, K.P., and T. Angelo. 1988. *Classroom Assessment Techniques: A Handbook for Faculty.* Ann Arbor, Mich.: National Center for Research to Improve Postsecondary Teaching and Learning, University of Michigan. ED 317 097. 166 pp. MF–01; PC–01.

Cuevas, G. 1991. "Feedback from Classroom Research Projects." *Community/Junior College* 15: 381–90.

Deming, W.E. 1982. *Out of Crisis.* Cambridge, Mass.: Massachusetts Institute of Technology.

Detmer, R. Spring 1994. "Teamwork in Teaching Using Computers: Quality Enhancement While Reducing Redundant Effort." *Culture of Quality: Faculty Showcase.* Maryville, Mo.: Northwest Missouri State University.

Dooris, M., and G. Lozier. Fall 1990. "Adopting Formal Planning Approaches: The Pennsylvania State University." In *Adapting Strategic Planning to Campus Realities,* edited by F. Schmidtlein and T. Milton. New Directions for Institutional Research No. 67. San Francisco: Jossey-Bass.

Dumaine, B. September 5, 1994. "The Trouble with Teams." *Fortune:* 86–92.

Eskes, D. Spring 1992. "Zero Defects: The College of Business Climbs aboard the TQM Express." *Business* 4(3): 16–19.

Ewell, P. May/June 1993. "Total Quality and Academic Practice: The Idea We've Been Waiting For?" *Change:* 49–55.

Fisher, R., and W. Ury. 1981. *Getting to Yes: Negotiating Agreement without Giving In.* New York: Penguin Books.

Freed, J., M. Klugman, and J. Fife. 1994. "Total Quality Management on Campus: Implementation, Experiences, and Observations." Unpublished manuscript. Tucson, Ariz.: ASHE Conference. ED 375 734. 24 pp. MF–01; PC–01.

Garvin, D. 1992. "A Note on Quality: Views of Deming, Juran, and Crosby." Harvard Business School Publication 9-687-001.

Gitlow, H., and S. Gitlow. 1987. *The Deming Guide to Quality and Competitive Position.* Englewood Cliffs, N.J.: Prentice-Hall.

Hamel, G., and C. Prahalad. Sept. 5, 1994. "Seeing the Future First." *Fortune:* 64–70.

Harris, J. 1992. "Key Concepts of Quality Improvement for Higher Education." In *Quality Quest in the Academic Process,* edited by J. Harris and J. Baggett. Methuen, Mass.: GOAL/QPC.

———. Summer 1993. "Samford University's Quality Story." In *Pursuit of Quality in Higher Education: Case Studies in Total Quality Management,* edited by D. Teeter and G. Lozier. San Francisco: Jossey-Bass.

Helminski, L. Fall 1992. "TQM in the Classroom." *Vision '92: The Maricopa Community College Journal of Teaching and Learning* 4(2): 10, 22.

Herrera, A. 1989. "A Survey of the Utilization of Classroom Research Techniques by Faculty and Administrators at Miami-Dade Community College." Unpublished manuscript. Miami: Miami-Dade Community College.

Hershauer, J. January 1994. "College of Business Undergraduate Committee Proposed Business Core Improvements." Unpublished internal document. Tempe, Ariz.: Arizona State University.

Hubbard, D. 1992. "TQM in Higher Education: Learning from the Factories." Unpublished draft document.

———. May 1994. "Can Higher Education Learn from Factories?" *Quality Progress.*

Hudson, M. 1992. "Statistical Thinking and Techniques: A General Education Requirement." In *Quality Quest in the Academic Process,* edited by J. Harris and J. Baggett. Methuen, Mass.: GOAL/QPC.

Hunsinger, R. 1992. "Total Quality Improvement in the Basic Sciences: A Retrospective Case Study." In *Quality Quest in the Academic Process,* edited by J. Harris and J. Baggett. Methuen, Mass.: GOAL/QPC.

Jennings, M., and T. Keller. May 5, 1994. "Memorandum on LES 579/ MGT 589." Unpublished internal document.

Johnson, J. Spring 1994. "Culture of Quality Links to Lifetime Wellness." *Culture of Quality Faculty Showcase.* Maryville, Mo.: Northwest Missouri State University.

Juran, J. 1964. *Managerial Breakthrough.* New York: McGraw-Hill.

Keller, G. 1983. *Academic Strategy: The Management Revolution in American Higher Education.* Baltimore: Johns Hopkins University Press.

Kennedy, L. 1991. *Quality Management*. San Francisco: Jossey-Bass.

Kerr, C., M. Gade, and M. Kawaoka. 1994. *Higher Education Cannot Escape History: Issues for the Twenty-First Century*. Albany, N.Y.: State University of New York.

Kohn, A. 1994. "Rewards in the 'Real World': The Workplace, the Classroom, and the Status Quo." *Cooperative Learning* 14(2): 20-23.

Koteen, J. 1989. *Strategic Management in Public and Nonprofit Organizations: Thinking and Acting Strategically on Public Concerns*. New York: Praeger.

Layzell, D., C. Lovell, and J. Gill. November 1994. "Developing and Viewing Faculty as an Asset for Institutions and States." Unpublished paper, ASHE annual meeting. ED 375 722. 19 pp. MF-01; PC-01.

Lomeli, R. Fall 1993. "Business Enrichment Program Evaluation." Unpublished internal document. Tempe, Ariz.: Arizona State University.

McCabe, R., and M. Jenrette. 1990. "Leadership in Action: A Campuswide Effort to Strengthen Teaching." In *How Administrators Can Improve Teaching*, by P. Seldin and Associates. San Francisco: Jossey-Bass.

McNeill, B. 1994a. *A Guide to Self-Evaluation of Educational States*. Tempe, Ariz.: College of Engineering and Applied Sciences, Mechanical and Aerospace Engineering Department, Arizona State University.

―――. 1994b. *Documentation of Technical Work: The Process and the Product*. Tempe, Ariz.: College of Engineering and Applied Sciences, Mechanical and Aerospace Engineering Department, Arizona State University.

McNeill, B., and L. Bellamy. 1994a. *Curriculum Development, Design Specifications, and Assessment*. Tempe, Ariz.: College of Engineering and Applied Sciences, Arizona State University. HE 028 425. 160 pp. MF-01; PC-07.

―――. 1994b. *Engineering Core Workbook: Active Learning, Team Training, and Assessment*. Tempe, Ariz.: College of Engineering and Applied Sciences, Arizona State University.

―――. 1995a. *A Guide to Self-Evaluation and Documentation of Educational States with Deviations*. Tempe, Ariz.: College of Engineering and Applied Sciences, Mechanical and Aerospace Engineering Department, Arizona State University. HE 028 423. 45 pp. MF-01; PC-02.

―――. 1995b. *Engineering Core Workbook for Active Learning, Assessment, and Team Training*. 2d ed. Tempe, Ariz.: Engineering Copy Service, Arizona State University. HE 028 428. 180 pp. MF-01; PC-08.

McPheters, L. April 1994. "From the Dean's Office." *MBA Council*

News 2(1).

Madden, C. Spring 1992. "A Diamond in the Rough." *Business* 4(3): 12–15.

Manz, C., and G. Stewart. May 1994. "Attaining Flexible Stability by Integrating Total Quality Management and Socio-Technical Systems Theory." Unpublished manuscript. Tempe, Ariz.: Arizona State University.

Marchese, T. May 1994. "Quality for the Long Haul." *AAHE Bulletin.*

Maricopa Community Colleges. 1994. *Information Update.*

Matthews, J. July 30, 1993a. "Award-Winning Educators Focus on Learning, Not Teaching." *ASU Insight:* 14(5).

———. Oct. 22, 1993b. "ASU Joins Coalition to Improve Engineering Education." *ASU Insight:* 14(17).

Matthews, W. January/February 1993. "The Missing Element in Higher Education." *Journal for Quality and Participation:* 102–8.

MBA Council News. June 1993. 1(1).

MBA Program Office. 1994. *MBA Program, Arizona State University.* Tempe, Ariz.: Arizona State University.

Miami-Dade Community College 1993–1994 Fact Book. 1993. Miami: Miami-Dade Community College.

Northwest Missouri State University. 1994a. *Application for the Missouri Quality Award.*

———. Jan. 6, 1994b. *Mini-Symposium Schedule.*

———. 1994c. *Undergraduate Academic Catalog 1994–1996.*

Numerof, R., and M. Abrams. December 1994. "How to Prevent the Coming Failure of Quality." *Quality Progress:* 93–97.

Pall, G. 1987. *Quality Process Management.* Englewood Cliffs, N.J.: Prentice-Hall.

Peters, T., and R. Waterman, Jr. 1982. *In Search of Excellence: Lessons from America's Best-Run Companies.* New York: Warner Books.

Poulton, N. 1980. "Strategies for Large Universities." In *Improving Academic Management,* by P. Jedamus, M.W. Peterson, and Associates. San Francisco: Jossey-Bass.

Quantum Quality Executive Council. January 1994. *First Annual Report on Quantum Quality.* Phoenix: Maricopa County Community College District.

Quinn, J. 1980. *Strategies for Change: Logical Incrementalism.* Homewood, Ill.: Irwin.

Rio Salado Community College. 1991a. *Adjunct Faculty Handbook.* Phoenix: Rio Salado Community College.

———. 1991b. *Total Quality Management Handbook.* Phoenix: Rio Salado Community College.

———. 1994a. *Catalog 1994–95.* Phoenix: Rio Salado Community College.

———. Summer/Fall 1994b. *Course Schedule.* Phoenix: Rio Salado

Community College.

———. 1994c. "TQM in the Classroom: Developing Practical Applications." Unpublished manuscript. Phoenix: Rio Salado Community College.

Roberts, H. 1990. *The Quality Revolution and the Business School Response.* Selected Paper No. 7. Chicago: The University of Chicago Graduate School of Business. HE 028 495. 28 pp. MF–01; PC–02.

———. 1992. "Personal Quality Checklists for Facilitation of Total Quality Management." Unpublished manuscript. Chicago: The University of Chicago.

———. 1993. "Grassroots TQM in Education: A Case History from Chicago." Unpublished manuscript. Chicago: The University of Chicago. HE 028 431. 24 pp. MF–01; PC–01.

Schuler, R., and D. Harris. 1992. *Managing Quality: The Primer for Middle Managers.* New York: Addison-Wesley.

Seymour, D. 1991. *Total Quality Management in Higher Education: A Critical Assessment.* Methuen, Mass.: GOAL/QPC.

———. 1992. *On Q: Causing Quality in Higher Education.* New York: American Council on Education/Macmillan Publishing.

———. May/June 1993. "Quality on Campus: Three Institutions, Three Beginnings." *Change:* 14–27.

———. January/February 1994. "The Baldrige Cometh." *Change:* 171.

Smith, G. Winter 1994. "Being a Business Student in the '90s Is Not Like You Remember." *Business.*

Smith, J. July 27, 1992. "Professor Finds Judging Quality Tough Task." *ASU Insight:* 5.

———. March 26, 1993a. "Business Recognizes Skills of Teaching Trio." *ASU Insight* 13(36): 3.

———. May 28, 1993b. "Hewlett-Packard Awards $100,000 Computer Grant to Business College for Teaching, Research." *ASU Insight* 13(45): 2.

———. Oct. 28, 1994. "Minority Enrollment Reaches 24 Percent in MBA Program." *ASU Insight* 15(18): 3.

Stewart, T. May 18, 1992. "The Search for the Organization of Tomorrow." *Fortune.*

———. Nov. 28, 1994. "How to Lead a Revolution." *Fortune:* 48–61.

Strickland, B. 1992. "Reducing the Hassle for Faculty through QI." In *Quality Quest in the Academic Process,* edited by J. Harris and J. Baggett. Methuen, Mass.: GOAL/QPC.

Teaching/Learning Project. Spring 1992. "Announcement of Award of First Endowed Chairs." Unpublished internal document. Miami: Miami-Dade Community College.

———. 1993. "Faculty Advancement System." Unpublished internal document. Miami: Miami-Dade Community College.

Teal, J. 1992. "Fear in the Classroom: Implications for Quality Improvement." In *Quality Quest in the Academic Process*, edited by J. Harris and J. Baggett. Methuen, Mass.: GOAL/QPC.

Teeter, D., and G. Lozier, eds. Summer 1993. *Pursuit of Quality Higher Education: Case Studies in Total Quality Management.* New Directions for Institutional Research No. 78. San Francisco: Jossey-Bass.

Thor, L. February 1993. "The Human Side of Quality: Employee Care and Empowerment." Paper presented at the League for Innovation in the Community College's Conference on Community Colleges and Corporations: Partners in Total Quality Management. Irvine, Calif. ED 354 044. 21 pp. MF–01; PC–01.

U.S. Department of Commerce. 1992. *The Malcolm Baldrige National Quality Awards: 1992 Award Criteria.* Gaithersburg, Md.: National Institute of Standards and Technology.

———. 1995a. *The Malcolm Baldrige National Quality Awards: 1995 Application Forms and Instructions.* Gaithersburg, Md.: National Institute of Standards and Technology.

———. 1995b. *The Malcolm Baldrige National Quality Awards: 1995 Application Forms and Instructions. Update.* Gaithersburg, Md.: National Institute of Standards and Technology.

———. 1995c. *The Malcolm Baldrige National Quality Awards: 1995 Education Pilot Criteria.* Gaithersburg, Md.: National Institute of Standards and Technology.

Waterman, R., Jr. 1987. *The Renewal Factor: How the Best Get and Keep the Competitive Edge.* New York: Bantam Books.

Weymuth, A. Oct. 14, 1994. Personal communique. Northwest Missouri State University.

Wolverton, M. December 1991. "You've Come a Long Way, Baby! Rio Salado Community College—Arizona's Shining Star." Unpublished manuscript. Tempe, Ariz.: Arizona State University.

———. 1994. "A Design for the Future: A Case Study of Miami-Dade Community College's Teaching/Learning Project." Unpublished manuscript. Tempe, Ariz.: Arizona State University.

———. 1995. "The College of Business at Arizona State University: Taking Quality to Heart." In *Total Quality in Higher Education: Academic Applications*, edited by H. V. Roberts. Milwaukee: ASQC Quality Press.

Zangwill, W., and H. Roberts. 1993. "Benchmarking Outstanding Leadership in Higher Education: Innovation Today and Tomorrow." Unpublished manuscript. Chicago: The University of Chicago. HE 028 430. 28 pp. MF–01; PC–02.

INDEX

used in evaluation of programs, 83
barrier-producing roles, 35
Bellamy, Lynn, 93
benchmarking, 84
benchmarks as targets instead of guides, 17
Bloom's taxonomy of cognitive learning, 43
Boeing CQI training program in Seattle, 42
    on basic precepts of team building, 48
Business Week report of alumni dissatisfaction, 79

C

case studies
    criteria used to select, 20
    sources of information for, 21
Chaffee
    central weakness of approach of, 10
    discourse on linear, adaptive and interpretive strategies,
        10
classroom feedback course results in emphasis shift
    from student achievement to teaching styles, 75
College of Engineering. See ASU or University of Chicago
competence matrix, 45, 47
constancy of purpose concept, 04
continuous improvement as only true route to improved quality,
    4
continuous quality improvement. See also quality principles
    as a short-term fix, 16-17
    Boeing training program in Seattle, 42
    characteristics common to all, 79-84
    characteristics of some quality efforts, 82-84
    classroom and curriculum, 80-81
    Commitment at the top: the role of leadership, 80
    cost in time and money, 81-82
    customer focus, 79-80
    Customized faculty development, 81
    faculty participation required, 89
    parallel between traditional CQI and classroom assessment,
        24
    perspective on, 3
    pursuing objectives without dialogue, methods or jargon,
        21
    misapplication in educational setting of, 16
    responsibility of top management, 5
    student-as-customer is greatest hurdle for advocates of, 19
    Teaching/Learning Project similarities to, 72
continuous quality improvement misgivings regarding
    Benchmarks and Customer Focus as limits on quality, 88
    Interdisciplinary Consequences, 88-89

first comprehensive electronic campus, 56
goals of student assessment procedures, 56
institutionwide instructional goals, 55
teaching workshops for new faculty at, 56
NWMSU. *See* Northwest Missouri State University

O
Oslo Business School in Norway, 33

P
Pareto
analysis, 61
charts, 62
diagrams, 25, 27
part-time coordinators used for quality coordinators, 82
Penley, Larry, 93
personal quality checklist, 25, 27
Phoenix College, 66, 69
Plan-Do-Check-Act cycle, charting a plan of action using, 61
poor quality costs, 6
problem free product requirements, 6
process verbs, definition of, 46
product quality improvement along five dimensions, 6

Q
quality
eight dimensions of, 13
defined through the eyes of the producer, 12
definition of Deming determined by producers & users, 13
index based on seven Baldrige criteria, 12
indicators, departments use of, 55
learning, principles of, 66-67
office, existence of, 82
philosophy in the service industry, 6
responsibility, 82
Quality and Operational Results criteria of Baldrige Award, 9
Quality and Productivity Improvement course, 22
Quality Leadership, elective course titled, 62
quality principles, x. *See also* SLI, CQI *and* TQL
required for curricula, faculty & administration, 87
various terms for, ix
Quantum Quality, 64, 80, 82
estimates for full institutionalization of, 70
motivation behind adoption of, 79

R
reflection log, 47

Z

zero defects as only acceptable performance standard, 6

ASHE-ERIC HIGHER EDUCATION REPORTS

Since 1983, the Association for the Study of Higher Education (ASHE) and the Educational Resources Information Center (ERIC) Clearinghouse on Higher Education, a sponsored project of the Graduate School of Education and Human Development at The George Washington University, have cosponsored the *ASHE-ERIC Higher Education Report* series. The 1994 series is the twenty-third overall and the sixth to be published by the School of Education and Human Development at the George Washington University.

Each monograph is the definitive analysis of a tough higher education problem, based on thorough research of pertinent literature and institutional experiences. Topics are identified by a national survey. Noted practitioners and scholars are then commissioned to write the reports, with experts providing critical reviews of each manuscript before publication.

Eight monographs (10 before 1985) in the ASHE-ERIC Higher Education Report series are published each year and are available on individual and subscription bases. To order, use the order form on the last page of this book.

Qualified persons interested in writing a monograph for the ASHE-ERIC Higher Education Reports are invited to submit a proposal to the National Advisory Board. As the preeminent literature review and issue analysis series in higher education, we can guarantee wide dissemination and national exposure for accepted candidates. Execution of a monograph requires at least a minimal familiarity with the ERIC database, including *Resources in Education* and *Current Index to Journals in Education.* The objective of these Reports is to bridge conventional wisdom with practical research. Prospective authors are strongly encouraged to call Dr. Fife at 800-773-3742.

For further information, write to
ASHE-ERIC Higher Education Reports
The George Washington University
1 Dupont Circle, Suite 630
Washington, DC 20036
Or phone (202) 296-2597, toll-free: 800-773-ERIC.
Write or call for a complete catalog.

ADVISORY BOARD

Barbara E. Brittingham
University of Rhode Island

Mildred Garcia
Montclair State College

Rodolfo Z. Garcia
North Central Association of Colleges and Schools

James Hearn
University of Georgia

Bruce Anthony Jones
University of Pittsburgh

L. Jackson Newell
Deep Springs College

Carolyn Thompson
State University of New York–Buffalo

CONSULTING EDITORS

C. Robert Pace
University of California–Los Angeles

James Rhem
The National Teaching & Learning Forum

Gary Rhoades
University of Arizona

Scott Rickard
Association of College Unions–International

G. Jeremiah Ryan
Harford Community College

Patricia A. Spencer
Riverside Community College

Frances Stage
Indiana University–Bloomington

Kala M. Stroup
Southeast Missouri State University

David Sweet
OERI, U.S. Dept. of Education

Barbara E. Taylor
Association of Governing Boards

Carolyn J. Thompson
State University of New York–Buffalo

Sheila L. Weiner
Board of Overseers of Harvard College

Wesley K. Willmer
Biola University

Manta Yorke
Liverpool John Moores University

REVIEW PANEL

Charles Adams
University of Massachusetts–Amherst

Louis Albert
American Association for Higher Education

Richard Alfred
University of Michigan

Henry Lee Allen
University of Rochester

Philip G. Altbach
Boston College

Marilyn J. Amey
University of Kansas

Kristine L. Anderson
Florida Atlantic University

Karen D. Arnold
Boston College

Robert J. Barak
Iowa State Board of Regents

Alan Bayer
Virginia Polytechnic Institute and State University

John P. Bean
Indiana University–Bloomington

John M. Braxton
Peabody College, Vanderbilt University

Ellen M. Brier
Tennessee State University

Barbara E. Brittingham
The University of Rhode Island

Dennis Brown
University of Kansas

Peter McE. Buchanan
Council for Advancement and
    Support of Education

Patricia Carter
University of Michigan

John A. Centra
Syracuse University

Arthur W. Chickering
George Mason University

Darrel A. Clowes
Virginia Polytechnic Institute and State University

Deborah M. DiCroce
Piedmont Virginia Community College

Cynthia S. Dickens
Mississippi State University

Sarah M. Dinham
University of Arizona

Kenneth A. Feldman
State University of New York–Stony Brook

Dorothy E. Finnegan
The College of William & Mary

Mildred Garcia
Montclair State College

Rodolfo Z. Garcia
Commission on Institutions of Higher Education

Kenneth C. Green
University of Southern California

James Hearn
University of Georgia

Edward R. Hines
Illinois State University

Deborah Hunter
University of Vermont

Philo Hutcheson
Georgia State University

Bruce Anthony Jones
University of Pittsburgh

Elizabeth A. Jones
The Pennsylvania State University

Kathryn Kretschmer
University of Kansas

Marsha V. Krotseng
State College and University Systems of West Virginia

George D. Kuh
Indiana University–Bloomington

Daniel T. Layzell
University of Wisconsin System

Patrick G. Love
Kent State University

Cheryl D. Lovell
State Higher Education Executive Officers

Meredith Jane Ludwig
American Association of State Colleges and Universities

Dewayne Matthews
Western Interstate Commission for Higher Education

Mantha V. Mehallis
Florida Atlantic University

Toby Milton
Essex Community College

James R. Mingle
State Higher Education Executive Officers

John A. Muffo
Virginia Polytechnic Institute and State University

L. Jackson Newell
Deep Springs College

James C. Palmer
Illinois State University

Robert A. Rhoads
The Pennsylvania State University

G. Jeremiah Ryan
Harford Community College

Mary Ann Danowitz Sagaria
The Ohio State University

Daryl G. Smith
The Claremont Graduate School

William G. Tierney
University of Southern California

Susan B. Twombly
University of Kansas

Robert A. Walhaus
University of Illinois–Chicago

Harold Wechsler
University of Rochester

Elizabeth J. Whitt
University of Illinois–Chicago

Michael J. Worth
The George Washington University

RECENT TITLES

1994 ASHE-ERIC Higher Education Reports

1. The Advisory Committee Advantage: Creating an Effective
   Strategy for Programmatic Improvement
   by Lee Teitel

2. Collaborative Peer Review: The Role of Faculty in Improving
   College Teaching
   by Larry Keig and Michael D. Waggoner

3. Prices, Productivity, and Investment: Assessing Financial Strategies in Higher Education
   by Edward P. St. John

4. The Development Officer in Higher Education: Toward an
   Understanding of the Role
   by Michael J. Worth and James W. Asp, II

5. The Promises and Pitfalls of Performance Indicators in Higher
   Education
   by Gerald Gaither, Brian P. Nedwek, and John E. Neal

1993 ASHE-ERIC Higher Education Reports

1. The Department Chair: New Roles, Responsibilities and
   Challenges
   Alan T. Seagren, John W. Creswell, and Daniel W. Wheeler

2. Sexual Harassment in Higher Education: From Conflict to
   Community
   Robert O. Riggs, Patricia H. Murrell, and JoAnn C. Cutting

3. Chicanos in Higher Education: Issues and Dilemmas for the
   21st Century
   by Adalberto Aguirre, Jr., and Ruben O. Martinez

4. Academic Freedom in American Higher Education: Rights,
   Responsibilities, and Limitations
   by Robert K. Poch

5. Making Sense of the Dollars: The Costs and Uses of Faculty
   Compensation
   by Kathryn M. Moore and Marilyn J. Amey

6. Enhancing Promotion, Tenure and Beyond: Faculty Socialization
   as a Cultural Process
   by William G. Tierney and Robert A. Rhoads

7. New Perspectives for Student Affairs Professionals: Evolving
   Realities, Responsibilities and Roles
   by Peter H. Garland and Thomas W. Grace

8. Turning Teaching Into Learning: The Role of Student Responsibility in the Collegiate Experience
   by Todd M. Davis and Patricia Hillman Murrell

1992 ASHE-ERIC Higher Education Reports

1. The Leadership Compass: Values and Ethics in Higher Education
   John R. Wilcox and Susan L. Ebbs

2. Preparing for a Global Community: Achieving an International Perspective in Higher Education
   Sarah M. Pickert

3. Quality: Transforming Postsecondary Education
   Ellen Earle Chaffee and Lawrence A. Sherr

4. Faculty Job Satisfaction: Women and Minorities in Peril
   Martha Wingard Tack and Carol Logan Patitu

5. Reconciling Rights and Responsibilities of Colleges and Students: Offensive Speech, Assembly, Drug Testing, and Safety
   Annette Gibbs

6. Creating Distinctiveness: Lessons from Uncommon Colleges and Universities
   Barbara K. Townsend, L. Jackson Newell, and Michael D. Wiese

7. Instituting Enduring Innovations: Achieving Continuity of Change in Higher Education
   Barbara K. Curry

8. Crossing Pedagogical Oceans: International Teaching Assistants in U.S. Undergraduate Education
   Rosslyn M. Smith, Patricia Byrd, Gayle L. Nelson, Ralph Pat Barrett, and Janet C. Constantinides

1991 ASHE-ERIC Higher Education Reports

1. Active Learning: Creating Excitement in the Classroom
   Charles C. Bonwell and James A. Eison

2. Realizing Gender Equality in Higher Education: The Need to Integrate Work/Family Issues
   Nancy Hensel

3. Academic Advising for Student Success: A System of Shared Responsibility
   Susan H. Frost

4. Cooperative Learning: Increasing College Faculty Instructional Productivity
   David W. Johnson, Roger T. Johnson, and Karl A. Smith

5. High School–College Partnerships: Conceptual Models, Programs, and Issues
   Arthur Richard Greenberg

6. Meeting the Mandate: Renewing the College and Departmental Curriculum
   William Toombs and William Tierney

7. Faculty Collaboration: Enhancing the Quality of Scholarship and Teaching
   Ann E. Austin and Roger G. Baldwin

8. Strategies and Consequences: Managing the Costs in Higher Education
   John S. Waggaman

1990 ASHE-ERIC Higher Education Reports

1. The Campus Green: Fund Raising in Higher Education
   Barbara E. Brittingham and Thomas R. Pezzullo

2. The Emeritus Professor: Old Rank - New Meaning
   James E. Mauch, Jack W. Birch, and Jack Matthews

3. "High Risk" Students in Higher Education: Future Trends
   Dionne J. Jones and Betty Collier Watson

4. Budgeting for Higher Education at the State Level: Enigma, Paradox, and Ritual
   Daniel T. Layzell and Jan W. Lyddon

5. Proprietary Schools: Programs, Policies, and Prospects
   John B. Lee and Jamie P. Merisotis

6. College Choice: Understanding Student Enrollment Behavior
   Michael B. Paulsen

7. Pursuing Diversity: Recruiting College Minority Students
   Barbara Astone and Elsa Nuñez-Wormack

8. Social Consciousness and Career Awareness: Emerging Link in Higher Education
   John S. Swift, Jr.

1989 ASHE-ERIC Higher Education Reports

1. Making Sense of Administrative Leadership: The 'L' Word in Higher Education
   Estela M. Bensimon, Anna Neumann, and Robert Birnbaum

2. Affirmative Rhetoric, Negative Action: African-American and Hispanic Faculty at Predominantly White Universities
   Valora Washington and William Harvey

3. Postsecondary Developmental Programs: A Traditional Agenda with New Imperatives
   Louise M. Tomlinson

4. The Old College Try: Balancing Athletics and Academics in Higher Education
   John R. Thelin and Lawrence L. Wiseman

5. The Challenge of Diversity: Involvement or Alienation in the Academy?
   Daryl G. Smith

6. Student Goals for College and Courses: A Missing Link in Assessing and Improving Academic Achievement
   Joan S. Stark, Kathleen M. Shaw, and Malcolm A. Lowther

7. The Student as Commuter: Developing a Comprehensive Institutional Response
   Barbara Jacoby

8. Renewing Civic Capacity: Preparing College Students for Service and Citizenship
   Suzanne W. Morse

1988 ASHE-ERIC Higher Education Reports

1. The Invisible Tapestry: Culture in American Colleges and Universities
   George D. Kuh and Elizabeth J. Whitt

2. Critical Thinking: Theory, Research, Practice, and Possibilities
   Joanne Gainen Kurfiss

3. Developing Academic Programs: The Climate for Innovation
   Daniel T. Seymour

4. Peer Teaching: To Teach is To Learn Twice
   Neal A. Whitman

5. Higher Education and State Governments: Renewed Partnership, Cooperation, or Competition?
   Edward R. Hines

6. Entrepreneurship and Higher Education: Lessons for Colleges, Universities, and Industry
   James S. Fairweather

7. Planning for Microcomputers in Higher Education: Strategies for the Next Generation
   Reynolds Ferrante, John Hayman, Mary Susan Carlson, and Harry Phillips

8. The Challenge for Research in Higher Education: Harmonizing Excellence and Utility
   Alan W. Lindsay and Ruth T. Neumann

*Out-of-print. Available through EDRS. Call 1-800-443-ERIC.

ORDER FORM

Quantity   **Amount**

_____ Please begin my subscription to the 1994 *ASHE-ERIC Higher Education Reports* at $98.00, 31% off the cover price, starting with Report 1, 1994. Includes shipping. _____

_____ Please send a complete set of the 1993 *ASHE-ERIC Higher Education Reports* at $98.00, 31% off the cover price. Please add shipping charge, below. _____

Individual reports are avilable at the following prices:
1993 and 1994, $18.00; 1988–1992, $17.00; 1980–1987, $15.00

SHIPPING CHARGES
For orders of more than 50 books, please call for shipping information.

	1st three books	Ea. addl. book
U.S., 48 Contiguous States		
Ground:	$3.75	$0.15
2nd Day*:	8.25	1.10
Next Day*:	18.00	1.60
Alaska & Hawaii (2nd Day Only)*:	13.25	1.40

U.S. Territories and Foreign Countries: Please call for shipping information.
*Order will be shipping within 24 hours of request.
All prices shown on this form are subject to change.

PLEASE SEND ME THE FOLLOWING REPORTS:

Quantity	Report No.	Year	Title	Amount

Please check one of the following:
☐ Check enclosed, payable to GWU–ERIC.
☐ Purchase order attached ($45.00 minimum).
☐ Charge my credit card indicated below:
    ☐ Visa   ☐ MasterCard

Subtotal: _____
Shipping: _____
Total Due: _____

Expiration Date _____

Name _____

Title _____

Institution _____

Address _____

City _____ State _____ Zip _____

Phone _____ Fax _____ Telex _____

Signature _____ Date _____

SEND ALL ORDERS TO: ASHE-ERIC Higher Education Reports
The George Washington University
One Dupont Cir., Ste. 630, Washington, DC 20036-1183
Phone: (202) 296-2597 • Toll-free: 800-773-ERIC